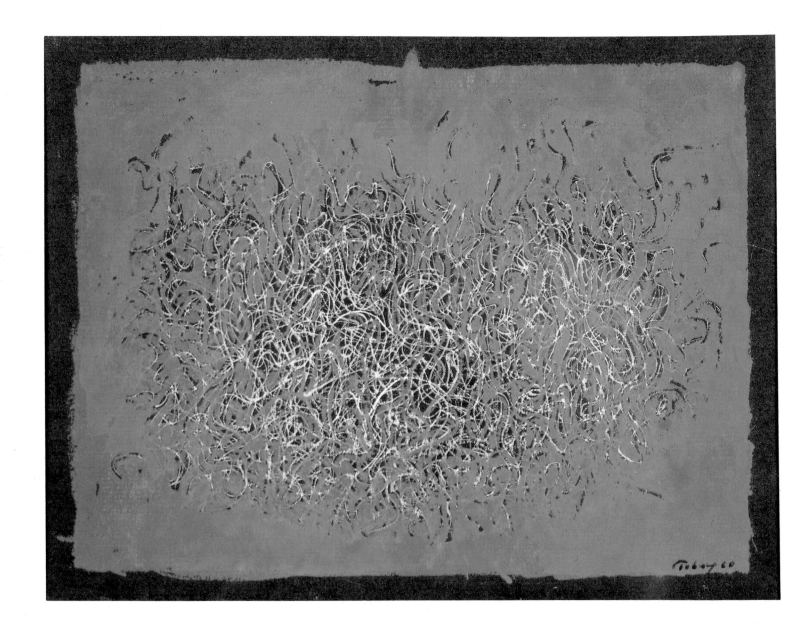

MARK TOBEY

Art and Belief

by Arthur L. Dahl and others

A collection of essays and other pieces
with 17 colour plates and 62 black-and-white plates

GEORGE RONALD · OXFORD

GEORGE RONALD, Publisher
46 High Street, Kidlington, Oxford

ISBN 0–85398–179–5 Hardcover
ISBN 0–85398–180–9 Softcover

Printed in Hong Kong

CONTENTS

Acknowledgements

The Publisher acknowledges with thanks permission from the following publishers to reprint extracts from: *Mark Tobey* by William C. Seitz, 1962, The Museum of Modern Art, New York, all rights reserved; *Tribute to Mark Tobey*, 1974, Smithsonian Institution Press, Washington DC, the catalogue of an exhibition held 7 June to 8 September 1974 at the National Museum of American Art, Smithsonian Institution; *The Bahá'í World*, Vol. XVI, 1978, Bahá'í World Centre, Haifa; *World Order*, 1, No. 5, August 1935 (The One Spirit), and 5, No. 1, April 1939 (Art and Community), The National Spiritual Assembly of the Baha'is of the United States, Wilmette, Illinois. The Publisher also thanks Roger White for permission to reprint his poem on Mark Tobey, and the Seattle Art Museum for permission to print the poems by Mark Tobey from his personal archives.

The Publisher thanks all the owners of works by Mark Tobey reproduced in this book for permission to do so. The Publisher also acknowledges with thanks the following for supplying photographs for the plates:
Rudolph Burckhardt, 54
Geoffrey Clements, 52, 66, 78
Colorphoto Hans Hinz, 3
Charles W. DeBus, 1
Leo Holub, 10, 58, 65, 71
Philippe Huneau, 9
M. Knoedler & Co., 5
Jerry Lebeck, 16
John H. Livingston, 56, 57
Janine Pradeau, 55
Robert Vinnedge, 18, 26, 68

Foreword

The purpose of this book is to illustrate a theme – the connection between the work of a major artist and his religious belief. The artist is Mark Tobey; the religion, the Bahá'í Faith. Although this book is not about the Bahá'í Faith, certain aspects of it are discussed and for the reader who knows nothing about it, there is a guide to further reading at the end of the book. As for Mark Tobey, it would not be possible to appreciate the theme of this book without some degree of knowledge of his life and work. Thus, although this book is neither biography nor art history, the reader will find much about the man, both public and private, and reproductions of many of his works, some well-known, some never illustrated before. Lest the reader should fear to find here the rigours of an academic dissertation, it is worth mentioning that this book was inspired by affection for a remarkable man and his exceptional creative achievement.

In the captions to the Plates, all dimensions are in inches, and height precedes width.

Several of the pieces have been published before, but for the most part they are not easily available. The Publisher is grateful for permission to reproduce these, as well as the paintings and drawings. It remains only to say that without the assiduous and enthusiastic help of Arthur L. Dahl this book could not have been published.

1926   1945   1963

MARK TOBEY, 1890–1976

by

Arthur L. Dahl

Mark Tobey occupies a unique position in the history of art: a painter of genius who also was deeply inspired through most of his productive life by the dynamic of a new religious impulse, the renewal of God's Word through Bahá'u'lláh. As a result, he has produced a body of work which has stirred controversy, been extraordinarily praised and grossly misunderstood, had a strong and still not fully comprehended influence on trends in art, and has helped a substantial number of people to become aware of the meaning and significance of the Bahá'í Faith.

His childhood years were much in the spirit of Tom Sawyer. He was born on 11 December 1890 in Centerville, Wisconsin, the youngest of four children of George Baker Tobey, a carpenter, house-builder and farmer, and Emma Jane (Cleveland) Tobey. The lineage was English, Welsh, German and Dutch.

In 1893 the family moved to near Jacksonville, Tennessee, where George Tobey built a house and intended to farm. Finding the educational facilities inadequate, they moved a year later to Trempealeau, Wisconsin, a village of 600 inhabitants on the banks of the Mississippi, where Mark spent the next twelve years as a typical Midwestern 'barefoot boy'. He studied and enjoyed nature avidly, excelled in those school subjects which interested him, attended the Congregational Church, and aspired in turn to being a minister, a taxidermist, a storekeeper and a trader. He recalled later: 'My whole experience until I was sixteen was just purely nature. Not the mind at all, just nature.'[1] His mother referred to him as 'the most restless young 'un I ever had,'[2] and that characteristic was manifest throughout his life. His family was devout, and a sense of religion was instilled early: 'I got my religion like my hair.'[3]

Little attention was paid to art in his school, but both of his parents were creative, his father making drawings and stone carvings of animals, and his mother weaving rugs. There is evidence that Tobey showed aptitude for art early, a fact noted by his family. After they moved to Hammond, Indiana in 1906 and it was evident that Mark was not interested in following his father into the building trade, his parents sent him to Saturday classes in watercolours and oils at the Art Institute of Chicago, the only formal art training he was to receive. One professor

Arthur Dahl was a friend of Mark Tobey from 1942 until the artist's death, and at one time had one of the largest private collections of his paintings. For eleven years he was Treasurer of the National Spiritual Assembly of the Bahá'ís of the United States. He lives in California.

1

there astutely characterized him as having 'the American handling bug', i.e. preferring flashy brush technique to the tedium of careful modelling.[4] After two years, however, Mark had to drop out of high school and seek work because of the illness of his father.

From 1909 to 1911, after the family moved to Chicago, Tobey changed jobs frequently. While working as a blueprint boy in a steel mill he studied mechanical drawing and spent his free time copying magazine covers. Several jobs later he was an errand boy for a fashion studio, where it was discovered he had a talent for drawing and he was engaged to draw the faces for catalogue illustrations at a substantial boost in salary. He clipped and studied the work of famous illustrators and portrait painters, and eventually discovered the great masters, first from prints, then from the originals at the Art Institute of Chicago.

By 1911 his confidence had grown to the point where he had settled in Greenwich Village, New York, determined to make good as a fashion illustrator. Indeed, he obtained a good job in this field with *McCall's Magazine*, and continued comparable work both in Chicago and New York for the next six years. In 1913 in Chicago he saw the famous 'Armory Show' but was not yet ready to penetrate the meaning of the radical works on display.

During this period Tobey's skill as a charcoal portraitist became recognized. He did portraits of many famous people, including Mary Garden, the opera star (his patroness for a while), Muriel Draper, Anthony Drexel Biddle and Governor Bell of New York, which were exhibited in a modern gallery run by Marie Sterner at M. Knoedler & Co. A year later Mrs Sterner was to change the course of his life. In Tobey's words:

'One night after an evening at a party at Marcel Duchamp's studio, while waiting for an elevated train I kept wondering if by chance there might be something else greater than art. This idea remained with me for several days — during which I thought considerably about the expression "the love of God", what it is, what it could mean to one like myself. This led to prayer to know about this profound state. After a short period of days I was called up by Mrs Sterner, who . . . asked me to dinner . . . That night in her beautiful house I sat beside a portrait painter named Juliet Thompson. After the evening was over we found we lived in the same direction. Fortunately, when we reached Fifth Avenue she said, "Let's walk." Since I didn't have ten cents in my pocket I couldn't have taken her on the bus very well. And so we walked, and before we parted she asked me to pose for her. Well, I had no money, nothing to do in particular, I owed my landlady forty dollars, so why not go and pose? . . .

'Upon a wall near where I was seated there was a photograph of a man with a white beard, wearing a white turban – a remarkable face, but I had no curiosity about him. During this period of posing I had a very strange and powerful dream which concerned this person in the photograph, or seemed to. When I told Miss Thompson about the dream she grew quite excited, but didn't say anything.

'After a while she decided to go to Green Acre. I took her to the train and upon leaving she said, "I have a plan for you; you will hear from me." After a week or so there came a letter from a man called Harry Randall, living in Little Boar's Head on the Maine coast. It contained $25 and an invitation to visit them, as they were friends of Miss Thompson. In Green Acre nearby there was a small group of Bahá'ís speaking of a new religion, claiming that the Day of Judgement was upon us and all the prophecies were now fulfilled. Also, I found out that Miss Thompson was a Bahá'í and had met the man in the photograph while he was in New York in 1912. Gradually it dawned on me that this little group of people with their prayers, their smiling faces and their unbounded enthusiasm regarding this new religion really had new spirit, anyway something I couldn't exactly put into

Plate 2 *Portrait of Martha Graham* 1928. Oil. $26\frac{1}{2} \times 19\frac{1}{2}$.
Collection Kendrick A. Schlatter, Los Angeles

words, but convinced me that what they believed was the truth.'[5]

So Mark Tobey accepted the Bahá'í Faith in 1918, and from that time on undertook a deep and continuous study of its teachings. Increasingly he felt moved to convey some of these exciting new spiritual concepts in his painting, but found it necessary to evolve new techniques to do so. William C. Seitz, whose essay in the catalogue for the Museum of Modern Art exhibition is the most profound analysis yet published of the impact of the Bahá'í Faith on Tobey's art, said: 'Without doubt, this [acceptance of the Bahá'í Faith] was the crucial spiritual redirection of Tobey's life and of his development as an artist.'[6] (Extracts from this essay, in two sections, are reprinted here, starting on page 13). Evidence was soon forthcoming in the painting *Conflict of the Satanic and Celestial Egos* (Plate 18), filled with metaphysical archetypes. However, another seventeen years were to pass before the real breakthrough occurred and Tobey discovered the principles and styles that were to be his great contributions to the progress of art in his age.

In 1919 Mark joined a Bahá'í study class organized by Albert Randall, which also included Lillian Randall, Juliet Thompson, Isobel F. Chamberlain, Mountfort Mills, Marjory Morten and Horace and Doris Holley, a number of them names well known to Bahá'ís. In October 1920 the class sent to 'Abdu'l-Bahá a prayer written by Horace Holley, and in December received in return a beautiful tablet which concluded: 'It was a touching melody and a supplication in the utmost sincerity. Rest ye assured that it will bring forth great fruits and thus inevitable confirmations will reach ye.'[7]

Coincidentally, a ferment was taking place in Tobey's approach to his art, particularly a reaction against 'the Renaissance sense of space and order'. He remembers that 'I really wanted to smash form, to melt it in a more moving and dynamic way.'[8] He was also storing up experiences that would surface later in many of his important paintings. The day World War I ended he walked the streets of New York with his friend Janet Flanner (who in future years was to write the famous *Letter from Paris* under the name 'Genet' in the *New Yorker*, and who first wrote of Mark's dedication to the Bahá'í Faith in a major article).[9] He recalls: 'You know, everything went wild. That's the only time I was ever lost in a fog.' These years were a montage of 'sirens, dynamic lights, brilliant parades and returning heroes. An age of confusion and stepped-up rhythms.'[10] Such visions can be seen in many of Tobey's city paintings as well as in some of the later abstractions.

In the early 1920s he became known for his caricatures of theatrical people, some of which were published in the *New York Times*, and for his drawings of vaudeville and burlesque personalities. A brief, unhappy marriage in 1922 and growing social demands caused him to want to get away from New York. A friend was returning home to Seattle and offered to share train space and a bag of oranges, so a new home was found. Seattle did not have the intellectual and cultural stimulation of New York, but it did offer spaciousness, great natural beauty, a slower, more relaxed pace, a diffuse light that has been likened to that of Paris, and some devoted, often discerning, friendships.[11] It also enabled Tobey to find a new activity that was to be a meaningful part of his artistic life for the next three decades: teaching. He was offered a post at the Cornish School, keeping 80¢ out of every $2.00 of tuition fees. He evolved a unique method of teaching, concentrating more on stimulating the imagination of the student, encouraging a love for art and overcoming the barrier of lack of confidence, than on following structured procedures and principles. Many of his students from both the Cornish School and his private classes have testified that he was a masterful teacher.

Mark claimed that he received as much from teaching as his students, and his own artistic development evolved in the process. In those Cornish years two important broadening events occurred. One was his personal discovery of cubism, as an outgrowth of his efforts to understand the work of such artists as Cézanne, Braque and Picasso. One night at the Cornish School, while working on a painting in a small, centrally lighted room, he imagined a fly moving about the room, crossing and recrossing its own path, its route forming a complex of line, with form being entirely the product of movement. This concept underlies much of his mature painting, but again it was years before he applied it.

The other event was his meeting in 1923 with Teng Kuei, a young Chinese artist studying at the University of Washington. They became close friends, and from Teng Mark learned both the technique and the philosophy of Chinese calligraphy. 'I have just had my first lesson in Chinese brush from my friend Teng Kuei,' Mark wrote. 'The tree is no more a solid in the earth, breaking into lesser solids bathed in chiaroscuro. There is pressure and release. Each movement, like tracks in the snow, is recorded and often loved for itself. The Great Dragon is breathing sky, thunder and shadow; wisdom and spirit vitalized.'[12] As Seitz puts it: 'What Tobey learned from Teng Kuei, but did not apply until later, was "the difference between volume and the living line" – a means of opening solid form, giving tangibility to empty space, and of breathing life into static Western realism.'[13]

Tobey also became interested in and collected the art of the Northwest and the Alaskan Indians. He had a strong sense of the value of indigenous art and culture. He also expressed sadness that the Pacific Coast did not look more towards the Orient for inspiration in its artistic expression, feeling that great opportunities were missed.

In 1925 he went to Europe, settling for several months in Paris. Then, in 1926 he accompanied friends to Spain, Greece, Turkey and the Lebanon, and later took advantage of the chance to make his first visit to the Bahá'í Shrines and World Centre at Haifa. After visiting the Shrine of Bahá'u'lláh he spent an hour with Shoghi Effendi, Guardian of the Bahá'í Faith: 'His grace when I first saw him is never to be forgotten, nor did he change when, years later, I had the opportunity to see him for a longer time . . . I made the Guardian laugh, which seemed to please him. Of course, in Haifa many things happen and yet all seems to melt in time which is no time. You are there – that's enough. Just to sit in a chair seems as important as going to town. You are released from yourself.'[14]

During the next three years Tobey divided his time between Seattle, New York and Chicago, teaching, experimenting and painting. An exhibit at a café gallery in New York caught the eye of Alfred H. Barr, Jr., who selected several of the paintings for an exhibition of American painters at the Museum of Modern

Mark Tobey's sketch of his 'personal discovery of Cubism'

Art. However, by 1930 the depression was threatening his position at the Cornish School. He was rescued when Mr and Mrs Leonard Elmhurst offered him a six-months' appointment as head of the painting department at Dartington Hall, a progressive school of the arts in Devonshire, about 200 miles from London, in the south-west of England.

Tobey stayed eight years. Here he associated with such intellectual leaders as Aldous Huxley, Rabindranath Tagore, Arthur Waley, Pearl Buck, the dancer Shankar, and the Jooss Ballet. He also formed a firm friendship wih the potter, Bernard Leach, which in time led to Leach's acceptance of the Bahá'í Faith. In 1932 further travels in Europe were made possible, and a second pilgrimage to the Bahá'í World Centre.

Another milestone for Tobey was reached in 1934, when the Elmhursts, seeing how close his friendship with Bernard Leach had become, gave Mark the funds to accompany Leach to the Orient. After a week in Hong Kong, absorbing the beauty and dynamism of that unique city, they separated, Mark stopping in Shanghai to spend time with his old friend Teng while Bernard went on to Japan. Shanghai gave Mark fresh impressions of the energy, the fascinating lines and textures to be found in the streets of a cosmopolitan city, and also the characteristics of Chinese life, culture and art. Such knowledge was extended still further when he went on to Japan and spent a month in a Zen monastery in Kyoto, studying calligraphy and painting, writing poetry and meditating.

This experience seemed to crystallize all the ideas and impressions he had been accumulating over the years. His previous work had been in a variety of styles and media, but was not disciplined and cohesive, tending towards what Muriel Draper called 'intellectualized philosophy in paint'.[15] But one evening in 1935 (or possibly 1936), after he had returned to Dartington Hall, he began to improvise a little picture very different from his others, a mesh of whitish lines on a brown background criss-crossing in a jumble of movement, somewhat like the flight of his imaginary fly. With sudden intuition he realized that he had been using the Chinese calligraphic impulse with a vision of the energy of the city, but that the result was occidental and was, in fact, New York. He called the painting *Broadway Norm*. In the next two or three nights he painted two more works in this idiom, larger and more significant, *Broadway* (page 19) and *Welcome Hero*. These three works represented the birth of his mature style and the discovery of a new language in art. He was 44 at the time.

Strangely enough, he did not immediately follow through with other important works in this style. Possibly he needed a more settled condition of life for a sustained outpouring of work. His first major museum show took place in 1935 at the Seattle Art Museum. He continued teaching at Dartington Hall and experimented with cubist still lifes. But the next significant move, and the beginning of his life as a mature artist, came in 1938 when, anticipating the outbreak of war, he returned to the United States and settled again in Seattle.

Initially he worked on a New Deal art project and taught painting in his studio. But he also began the creation of vitally original paintings incorporating the new 'white writing' technique on which his early fame rests. Most of the characteristic 'white writing' works were painted in the 1940s, when he was in his fifties, or later. The works with Bahá'í themes and titles were mostly done in the late 1940s and early 1950s. The Sumi paintings, very different from his other works, but in Tobey's judgement among his most significant contributions, were created in 1957, when he was 66. The experimentation with monotypes, which went on for more than a decade, began just before the Louvre exhibition in 1961. Though the works that initially made him famous were usually small in scale (and because of their size and subtlety do not always reproduce well), he did produce some

Plate 3 *Saggitarius Red* 1963. Oil, ink and crayon. $83\frac{1}{2} \times 152\frac{3}{4}$. Oeffentliche Kunstsammlung, Kuntsmuseum, Basel

large paintings in the 1960s and 1970s. And throughout all this period he would occasionally produce a representational work, including a notable series of self-portraits. In addition he maintained a lively interest in graphics.

Tobey was constantly trying new things, never content to mine a popular or saleable style. He once wrote: 'Artists don't repeat but always change as nature does.'[16] And later: 'I can't just paint for money or to please.'[17]

Tobey was fortunate in his dealers although acceptance and financial success came slowly. In 1939 he was introduced to Marian Willard (now Marian Willard Johnson) of the Willard Gallery in New York, who bought *Broadway*. In 1942 this painting won a competition at and was acquired by the Metropolitan Museum of Art. The Willard Gallery presented its first Tobey exhibition in 1944, and offered them frequently in subsequent years. He was first represented in the United States section of the Venice Biennale in 1948, and in 1951 Jermayne MacAgy organized his first big Retrospective at the Palace of the Legion of Honor in San Francisco, which travelled to the Whitney Museum in New York. In 1952 a twenty-minute film, *Mark Tobey*, highly subjective, experimental and sensitive, directed by Robert Gardner and with Tobey reading his poetry on the sound-track, redolent with Bahá'í concepts of oneness, was shown at the film festivals of Venice and Edinburgh. Otto Seligman became his dealer in Seattle and held his first one-man exhibition in 1954. Tobey's international reputation began in 1955 with his first showing at the Galerie Jeanne Bucher in Paris, and was further extended when he was represented by the Galerie Beyeler in Basel. In recent years the Foster/White Gallery has represented Mark in Seattle. The high regard with which he was held in Europe in the late 1950s was demonstrated by his being awarded the international prize for painting at the Venice Biennale in 1958. No other American had won it since Whistler, in 1895.

In 1960 Tobey made a change he had been contemplating for a long time, moving with his close friend Pehr Hallsten and his secretary Mark Ritter from Seattle to Basel, in Switzerland, settling in a charming, 500-year-old house with spacious rooms, in the old section of the city. The destruction of the beauties of the past in American cities in the name of progress, the accelerating pace of life and the interference with privacy that accompanied fame, made him feel the atmosphere in America had become stifling and no longer suitable for doing the important work he felt lay before him.

In 1961 the Musée des Arts Décoratifs, the modern wing of the Louvre in Paris, offered a monumental one-man Tobey exhibition containing 286 works, largely through the efforts of François Mathey, a Conservateur there and a strong champion of Tobey. Mark was the first living artist who was not French ever to be so honoured, and for the occasion the museum made major alterations in the huge rooms to accommodate the small, intimate scope of Tobey's paintings. This was followed by a smaller show at the Whitechapel Gallery in London, and the next year by a major exhibition at the Museum of Modern Art in New York, which travelled to Chicago and Cleveland.

Curiously enough, while many European critics considered Tobey the foremost living American painter, and although his work had a strong influence upon many artists in Europe, he was regarded with disdain by many of the New York critics and art magazines, which either ignored or played down the honours showered upon him abroad. Possibly it was provincialism, or a lack of empathy for the spiritual basis which underlay Tobey's search for new means of expression in painting, a very different basis from that which inspired the major figures in abstract expressionism. It is not surprising that lately several critics have expressed the need for a thorough study of the relative influence of Mark Tobey and Jackson Pollock on the art of their age, and on each other.

During the 1960s Tobey enlarged the size of his canvases, realizing that this was what museums were demanding. From this came a magnificent work in the densely packed style for which he is famous, seven feet tall, almost thirteen feet wide, *Sagittarius Red* (page 7), now in the Kunstmuseum, Basel, painted just after he returned from the Bahá'í World Congress at the Royal Albert Hall in London, in 1963, when he was 72 years old. Many consider this his masterpiece, and one of the towering paintings of the twentieth century. Shortly afterwards he created a large and controversial collage mural for the Seattle Opera House.

Tobey was accorded several other major exhibitions in the 1960s: one in 1966, organized by the Stedelijk Museum, Amsterdam, moving to Düsseldorf, Hanover and Bern; one in Dallas in 1968; and a celebration of Tobey's 80th birthday in Seattle in 1970, with exhibitions at the Seattle Art Museum, the Henry Gallery of the University of Washington and several commercial galleries. Unfortunately, Tobey's health did not permit him to attend. Exquisite smaller shows were held during this period at Stanford University and Honolulu.

The crowning moment, however, was an exhibition in 1974 at the National Collection of Fine Arts, a division of the Smithsonian Institution, Washington, DC, called 'Tribute to Mark Tobey'. Consisting of seventy works, more than half painted within fifteen years of the exhibition, or after Tobey was 67 years of age, it was an amazing testimony to Mark's creativity and stamina at an advanced age, and a confirmation of his judgement when he moved to Europe in 1960 that some of his greatest accomplishments lay ahead. (The introduction to the catalogue is reprinted here, starting on page 27.)

Though Mark was plagued by illness during a good part of his later years, his productivity continued unimpaired until about three years before his death, when the trauma of an operation affected his mind and restricted his capacity to paint.

During his years of productivity Tobey was continually faced with the problem of how to divide his time and energy between his art and direct service to the Bahá'í Faith. Certainly he made many important contributions to his Faith. While he lived in England at Dartington Hall he served on the British National Spiritual Assembly. In the years at Seattle he served on the Local Spiritual Assembly and once moved briefly to Victoria, in British Columbia, to prevent the membership of the Local Spiritual Assembly there from falling below the prescribed minimum. While in Switzerland he was chairman of the Spiritual Assembly of Basel for sixteen years. He gave numerous lectures and informal discussions, and took advantage of special opportunities to talk on the Faith, such as on an ocean voyage (he feared aeroplanes and took alternative means of transport wherever possible). During his years in Seattle he frequently attended the Geyserville Bahá'í School in California, which he loved, where he talked both formally and informally, but always eloquently, making art come alive and giving many Bahá'ís their first glimpse of the meaning and purpose of abstract art. He published three articles in the Bahá'í magazine, *World Order*. (Two of these are reprinted here.)

Though his financial circumstances were limited until he was almost 70, he was generous in assisting the Faith once international recognition had improved the market for his paintings. At one point he subsidized a pioneer teacher, and at another he donated the proceeds from the sale of ten important paintings to the National Spiritual Assembly of the United States.

Possibly his largest service to the Faith was the indirect one of being so much in the public eye in his later years, and identified as a Bahá'í. After 1955 almost every article, interview or book about him (some of which are in reference works that will be used for decades) mentioned the Faith and usually outlined those Bahá'í principles which had specific application to his art. Some studies went into this

Plate 4 *The Spinster* Tempera. $6\frac{3}{4} \times 4\frac{3}{4}$. Collection Eli Rashkov, Seattle

subject quite deeply, notably the fine essay by William C. Seitz previously referred to. A recent doctoral thesis by Frederic G. Hoffman, which may be published in another form in the future, also deals at length with the impact of the Bahá'í Faith on Tobey's art.

Tobey himself was realistic and objective in evaluating his own painting. He resisted being categorized as belonging to any 'school' of art. He believed in the excellence and lasting qualities of his work, but had no illusions of it representing a summit or climax of any period in art history. Rather he felt he was a link in an ongoing process. He opposed the use of the label 'Bahá'í artist', preferring to consider himself an artist who also happened to be a Bahá'í, and who was more profoundly influenced than most by the spirit and teachings of his religion. In a letter of 1963 he wrote: 'You know the Guardian freed art before his death,' then referring to Shoghi Effendi's remarks about 'Bahá'í art': 'There is no official Bahá'í Art, as this is not a new religion, but religion renewed.'

Mark participated in several international conferences on the arts, at which he either spoke of the Bahá'í Faith directly, or referred to some of its principles. These included the Western Round Table on Modern Art in San Francisco in 1949, participated in by Frank Lloyd Wright, Marcel Duchamp, Arnold Schoenberg and Gregory Bateson, and a Unesco conference, 'Artists from Eastern and Western Countries', in Vienna in 1960.

Numerous honours flowed to Mark after he reached his mid-sixties. In 1956 he was elected to the National Institute of Arts and Letters, and won the US National Prize in the Guggenheim International Award. In 1957 he was awarded the American Institute of Architects' Fine Arts Medal. In 1958, in addition to the top prize at the Venice Biennale, he won the first 'Art In America' award. In 1960 he was elected a member of the American Academy of Arts and Sciences, but did not accept the election. In 1961, at the time of the Louvre exhibition, he won first prize at the Carnegie Institute's 'Pittsburgh International Exhibition of Contemporary Painting and Sculpture'.

Tobey had a strong and memorable personality, and made a legion of devoted friends, both within the Bahá'í Faith and in the world at large. His conversation was brilliant on a variety of topics, and talking was one of his great pleasures. Taking a walk with Mark was a stimulating experience, for his powers of observation were acute and he could see meaning and beauty in the most commonplace objects. An unforgettable memory of this writer was standing with Tobey in one of the great redwood forests of Northern California, sensing his response to the cathedral majesty of the noble trees with the sun filtering between their massive trunks. He also had an encyclopaedic knowledge of Western art, and was a superb companion in a museum. As the critic Katherine Kuh wrote: 'My wanderings at the Kunstmuseum with Tobey reinforced a conviction I have long held – that artists are often better critics than professional ones. Aware of what makes their own work tick, certain painters can identify more clairvoyantly with colleagues who react to parallel stimuli. Little affected by popular opinion or intellectual snobbism, these men are satisfied by the making of art and hence do not depend on criticism for personal aggrandizement. What they accept is as revealing and often as astute as what they reject.'[18]

Tobey also loved people from all walks of life, and enjoyed observing such teeming and natural urban scenes as the famous Pike Market in Seattle, which inspired some memorable drawings and also figured prominently in the 1952 film. His humanity was particularly apparent in his close personal relationships, such as with his Swedish friend Pehr Hallsten. They were devoted to each other for more than twenty years, but it was not always easy for Mark. Since Pehr suffered from diabetes and often needed special attention and was difficult to deal with, he sometimes brought out the irascible side of Mark's nature. But Mark needed this outlet for his urge to nurture, and took wonderful care of Pehr. He encouraged Pehr to take up painting, believed he had a very strong sense of colour and an attractive primitive style, drawing on his memories of his childhood and knowledge of Swedish mythology. Mark was very proud of his several one-man shows. When Pehr died, Mark was inconsolable for many months.

Tobey's creativity extended to the other arts. He wrote a considerable amount of poetry, very sensitive and spiritually intuitive. He also enjoyed playing the piano, and composed several works for it and other instruments. A piano solo and a flute solo from his pen were included on the sound-track of the 1952 film.

Mark Tobey's long and productive life was an unending search to find and understand his inner self, and to reconcile the spiritual and the material. He could appreciate and respond to the physical beauties of the world to an extraordinary degree, yet he was always aware that there was much more than this, and his painting stretched to discover new means and dimensions of expression and vision, offering special insight in our eternal quest to grasp the nature of reality. Tobey once said: ' . . . we have occupied ourselves too much with the outer, the objective, at the expense of the inner world wherein the true roundness lies.'[19]

Mark Tobey died in his sleep on 24 April 1976, at his home in Basel. The funeral was held at St Alban's Church not far away, with about 150 people in attendance. Two of Mark's own musical compositions were played. A eulogy by Virginia Barnett, a close personal friend from Seattle and wife of Mark's attorney, contained these words: 'He could be both teacher and student. He could both give and receive friendship. He was generous in money and time and encouragement to young and old, while also sharply discriminating in terms of character and values . . . He was touchingly human, vulnerable, tender, proud, irascible, forgiving – and in my view, a ranking creative genius of this century.'[20]

In a cable of 26 April 1976 announcing his passing, the Universal House of Justice, the supreme institution of the Bahá'í Faith, referred to him as a 'distinguished dedicated servant [of] Bahá'u'lláh.'

TOBEY'S WORLD VIEW

by

William C. Seitz

*The earth has been round for some time now, but not
in man's relations to man nor in the understanding of
the arts of each as a part of that roundness. As usual we
have occupied ourselves too much with the outer, the
objective, at the expense of the inner world wherein the
true roundness lies.*[1]
*I remember when I saw a water spider and it brought
down a bubble of air and placed it over its nest – a
magical and fantastic thing. — Mark Tobey.*

Mark Tobey's paintings are seldom large, and many
are smaller than this page. They are usually rendered
in tempera or watercolour rather than oil, in unas-
sertive colours. His surfaces are worked with brush
strokes that can be explosively bold, but are more
often as delicate as the strands of a spider web or as
ephemeral as smoke rising from a cigarette. At first

---

*William C. Seitz was Curator of Painting and Sculp-
ture Exhibitions at the Museum of Modern Art, in
New York, and the two essays published here are
extracts from his important catalogue of the exhibition
of Tobey's works arranged by him in New York,
Cleveland and Chicago in 1962-3. Other posts he
held were Professor of Fine Arts and Director of the
Rose Art Museum at Brandeis University, and
Professor of Art History at the University of Virginia.*

some of his works seem two-dimensional, but if one
is willing to look long enough, the eye and mind are
led to enter a unique world of form, space and
meaning. One discovers, sometimes quite unex-
pectedly, that the smallest and least arresting work
can become vast in depth, extent, and significance.
The difference between the actual size and potential
scale of Tobey's pictures can be startling. Recalled in
memory, if one knows them well, they combine and
expand to define a spherical universe of forms and
ideas.

Before anything else, a work of art should
command attention as an energized object. The ideas
that engendered it must have been fused with their
medium to form a new substance. For this reason it is
often wrongly demanded that a painting decant its
entire meaning at a glance. Tobey's world of ideas
must be entered through his paintings, but they can
be fully understood only through familiarity with the
experiences and convictions that surround them. For
this reason his thought will be studied here before the
forms, and even the subjects of the paintings. This
sequence will exemplify the thinking behind Tobey's
brush, and demonstrate the interpenetration of his art
and life.

The artist, as Tobey realizes, is not a cool-headed
intellectual: 'What supremely rational person', he

Plate 5 *New Crescent* 1953. Tempera.
$23\frac{1}{2} \times 17\frac{1}{2}$. Private Collection

asks, 'can keep from going to sleep?'[2] With amusement – but not wholly in jest – he notes that journalists have called him a 'Northwest mystic', and 'the sage of Seattle'. Although current thought craves extrarational experience, it distrusts living saints, mystics, or prophets; and Tobey has never claimed such a status. Nonetheless, to deal with his views accurately one must recognize that they are often mystical and religious. Like Kandinsky, Klee, and Mondrian, Tobey sees the highest reality as spiritual rather than physical. His world view – properly so called because it is more embracing than the metaphysics of the three European painters – is theological as well as aesthetic. Tobey readily acknowledges the debt his art owes to his religion. Although he painted before his conversion to the Bahá'í World Faith in 1918, the existing content of his art is a direct outcome of this revelation. The premises of Bahá'í doctrine which support and permeate his thinking can be reduced to three interrelated concepts: unity, 'progressive revelation', and humanity.

. . . Bahá'í provided Tobey with aesthetic as well as social and religious principles. He has often stated that there can be no break between nature, art, science, religion, and personal life. The belief in an ultimate unity – visualized as a central focus or enclosing sphere, conceived as a common underlying substance as in early Greek monism or modern physics, known through an irrefutable experience as in mystical religion, or derived from a universal principle as in Buddhism – underlies a great body of human speculation. Few religions, however, have given the concept of *oneness* such pointed emphasis, and few modern artists have dealt with it as explicitly as has Tobey. Its most dramatic impact on his world view lies in the Bahá'í reversal of Kipling's dogma, 'East is East, and West is West, and never the twain shall meet,' by the conviction that 'all humanity whether it be in the East or in the West may be connected through the bond of this divine affection;

for we are all the waves of one sea.'[3] 'The East and West will embrace as long-lost lovers,' Tobey predicts, quoting Bahá'u'lláh.

As a 'universal' religion, Bahá'í recognizes a progression of prophets, martyrs, saints, and teachers of various faiths, culminating with Bahá'u'lláh but including Abraham, Moses, Zoroaster, Buddha, Christ, and Mohammed. Each is held to be the bearer of a common truth cast in the form that served the needs of a particular time and situation. As 'Abdu'l-Bahá emphasized when he lectured in the United States in 1912, the radical concept of 'progressive revelation' carries with it an identification with advanced opinion and knowledge in all fields of thought: 'Religion is the outer expression of the divine reality. Therefore it must be living, vitalized, moving and progressive. If it be without motion and non-progressive it is without divine life; it is dead . . . All things are subject to divine re-formation. This is a century of life and renewal. Sciences and arts, industry and invention have been reformed. Law and ethics have been reconstituted, reorganized. The world of thought has been regenerated. Sciences of former ages and philosophies of the past are useless today. Present exigencies demand new methods of solution; world problems are without precedent. Old ideas and modes of thought are fast becoming obsolete . . . for this is clearly the century of a new life, the century of the revelation of the reality and therefore the greatest of all centuries.'[4]

'Abdu'l-Bahá cites the progress of 'this radiant century' – 'the century of motion, divine stimulus and accomplishment' – 'the century of light' – as evidence that 'the new day' is at hand: 'The East and West can communicate instantly. A human being can soar in the skies or speed in submarine depths. The power of steam has linked the continents . . . Day by day discoveries are increasing. What a wonderful century this is!'[5]

There is a terrible alternative, however. With amazing insight for the period before World War I,

'Abdu'l-Bahá cites the destructiveness of modern armaments, and warns that 'if we remain fettered and restricted by human inventions and dogmas, day by day the world of mankind will be degraded, day by day warfare and strife will increase and satanic forces converge toward the destruction of the human race.'[6] Tobey's very early *Conflict of the Satanic and Celestial Egos* (Plate 18), painted shortly after his introduction to Bahá'í and influenced by Michelangelo and William Blake, depicts this struggle, as, in contemporary terms, does *The Void Devouring the Gadget Era* (Plate 35).

Except for the eschatological warning, the parallel between 'Abdu'l-Bahá's progressivism and early avant-garde writings such as Apollinaire's *The Cubist Painters* is striking. Even before Tobey's belated familiarity with advanced modern art, Bahá'í doctrine propelled him toward innovation, and surely lies behind the following statements: 'At a time when experimentation expresses itself in all forms of life, search becomes the only valid expression of the spirit . . .'[7] 'I am accused often of too much experimentation, but what else should I do when all other factors of man are in the same condition? I thrust forward into space as science and the rest do. The gods of the past are as dead today as they were when Christianity overcame the pagan world. The time is similar, only the arena is the whole world.'[8]

Tobey has sometimes been loosely regarded as an apostle of Zen. The error is apparent in comparing the 'oneness' of Zen with that of Bahá'í. Zen is not a religion, nor is it a pantheism or mysticism in the Western sense. Inherently anti-intellectual and anti-theoretical, it can have no theology. Differentiation between God and nature, nature and man, reason and emotion it regards as absurd. Bahá'í, by contrast, is totally anthropocentric and Western, though it originated in Persia. Criticized from a Zen viewpoint, indeed, Bahá'í is dualistic, dividing reality into parts.[9] Not only does Bahá'í theory separate godlike man from nature: it distinguishes natural law, as a controlling force, from the creatures it is held to direct. Beings 'lower' than human are 'captives of nature',[10] for the animal is unable to deviate from patterns of instinct and desire. Man, because he is endowed with intellect, reason, and spiritual powers, can probe the mysteries of nature, control natural law and even deviate from it. He is therefore not a part of nature but its ruler: 'higher and nobler by reason of the ideal and heavenly force latent and manifest in him.'[11]

As an artist, and because of his knowledge of Oriental art and Zen, Tobey finds a closer affinity of man to nature. Augmented from many other quarters, Bahá'í views on unity, humanity, and progressive revelation nevertheless operate in every phase of Tobey's painting after 1920, and he has painted many explicitly religious subjects. Inasmuch as Bahá'í upholds the innate truth of all religions, some paintings interpret Christian themes such as *The Last Supper, Homage to the Virgin, The Deposition* and *The Flight into Egypt.* Though deeply concerned with their significance, Tobey transforms them as a composer might an earlier musical form, motif, or specific composition; upon or into the ancient subject he builds 'a modern complex structure'.[12] More general in theme, *Western Splendor* (1943), 'a façade in grays and ambient light', is 'a wall of memories of churchly splendor surviving the ages.'[13]

Another group of religious paintings is specifically related to Bahá'í. Because he draws on a doctrine without an iconic tradition, Tobey is free to visualize the words of the Bahá'í spokesmen freely, and to originate his own pictorial conventions. Most important among this group, perhaps, are the works depicting martyrs, prophets, and the idea of progressive revelation. *The Cycle of the Prophet* deals with the rhythmic sequence of divine spokesmen; *Movement around the Martyr* celebrates the rebirth that follows his sacrifice as it takes form in social change, great music, art, and architecture; *The Retreat of the Friend* concerns the quiet retirement of the saint and friend of mankind as he makes way for another; *The Gold of the Martyr* contrasts spiritual with material wealth: *The New Day* (Plate 39) designates the period when peace reigns, and 'the sun of arts and crafts is manifest from the horizon of the heaven of the Occident.'[14]

Tobey's religious paintings, like those of Rouault, are noteworthy not only because he is a truly contemporary artist, but because they arise from conviction rather than as commissioned church decorations. He is venerated by the Bahá'í movement as their only great artist, but when asked, after a lecture at one of their meetings, about an official 'Bahá'í art', Tobey replied that modern literacy has made didactic art unnecessary, and that 'art would be free in a Bahá'í world.'[15]

Meyer Schapiro once observed that works of art are the 'last handmade, personal objects' left in our industrialized world.[16] It could also be said that artists are among the few professionals whose lives, personalities, and beliefs are organically integrated. Tobey believes in inspiration and intuition. 'Mankind today', he complains, quoting Bahá'u'lláh, 'has lost the power of scent.'[17] Tobey's likes and dislikes, ethics, religion, amusements, goings and comings, aesthetics — his very faults and weaknesses — make up one entity, whole and clearly defined even in its contradictions.

World-famous and no longer young, Tobey is as independent, volatile, and unpredictable as he must have been as a tyro fashion illustrator in his twenties. Now, as then, he is a romantic figure. No one, observing the white hair billowing back from his high forehead or the closely trimmed beard that shapes his chin, or catching a glimpse of him in the street wearing a rough tweed coat and a beret, could fail to realize that he is an artist. The image of Tobey wandering in the crowded streets of New York, Paris, Hong Kong, or Seattle, his senses alive to passers-by, buildings, weather, smells and sounds, pausing to observe them with curiosity, amusement,

and annoyance replacing each other in his mind, is both accurate and symbolic. Movement – or, more specifically, *migration* – is a leitmotiv of Tobey's life and art. He is fascinated by the skid-row drifters that haunt the Pike Place Public Market in Seattle; in part, perhaps, because he also has been a migrant, as restless as one of the twisting or drifting brush signs that activate the space of his paintings. Tobey's quest, like that of Bahá'í, is for peace – for the freedom and tranquility to paint and meditate. He dislikes crowds; but who has painted them with more understanding? He is a bad traveller, nervous in automobiles, uncomfortable in trains, and ill at ease in airplanes; but who has painted man's wanderings so meaningfully? As a friend once remarked, Tobey seems to paint what he most professes to dislike.

Tobey is an amateur musician and composer who plays the piano to relax and clarify his visual imagination; he has written expressive prose and good poetry, and is an insatiable reader of novels, poetry, books on botany, biology and travel, mystery stories, or whatever is at hand. He loves the film, concerts, and the theatre. His memory is boundless. Tobey's physical and spiritual migrations, therefore, have grown into an inexhaustible store of ideas and images, with facets widely separated in origin. The position of an initial impression in the whole is established slowly, as if maturation were essential for spirit and form to adjust to each other.

For an artist caught in the whirlpool of modern life a degree of egoism is essential for survival. Tobey knows that one cannot escape the limitation of the self – that 'you are you whether walking backward or forward',[18] but his art is directed outward: 'Oh, Tobey, he's always interested in nature, but I'm interested in myself,' a painter-friend complained. Tobey sees the ego, in its selfishness and separateness, as a limitation to be transcended: '"The era of adolescence is over."[19] We must concentrate outside ourselves. As we arrive at maturity we must take on new responsibilities. We all feel a separateness – we wish that a drop of water would soften our ego.'[20]

Tobey's thinking organizes itself through a series of contradictions or, perhaps better, oppositions. He admires modern science, but feels we are blinded by its achievements, and he is suspicious of psychology and psycho-analysis, because they have led us to obsession with psychic pressures: 'Focused almost completely on this, we forget that there are today great men in the religious field with as much to offer.'[21] He believes our society overvalues comfort, money, and possessions, with a result that is mechanizing and dehumanizing: 'We worship the young. We want *so* much muscle power for *so* much money.' He sees a strange belief in the 'immortality of the body... We're in the age of denial of everything but physical existence. The thing we've got to fight for is humanism – it's the highest thing we know; we can't mechanize ourselves out of existence.'[22] When drawn together, Tobey's scattered criticisms of modern life constitute an admonition depicting a society which, like that of Rome in the fourth century, is at a crossroad: one direction is toward fulfilment and the other toward extinction. When the question was raised, during a symposium in 1949, whether anyone in ancient Rome knew their culture was in decline, Tobey commented: 'I presume there were some, but they were called Christians.'[23] It is in this light that *Imperator* (Plate 30), which depicts a cracking Constantinian head, should be interpreted.

In the struggle between the spiritual and the material the United States, and especially New York, is a major battlefield. Very recently a French interviewer, discerning two currents, one active and the other contemplative, in Tobey's art, drew from him the following comment on his paintings of cities: 'No doubt I did them because I am an American painter. I cannot be indifferent to the swarming crowds, multitudes, neon signs, movie theatres, to the noises that I hate of modern cities.'[24] Tobey painted *Broadway* (page 19) amid the misty groves of Devonshire: 'Of course when I did *Broadway* I did it because I loved it, because I had experienced it. It was in my bones, but I could paint it best when I was farthest from it.' In New York, as elsewhere in America, however, Tobey sees the colour, individuality, camaraderie, fantasy, and tradition that pleased him disappearing. Double-decked buses on Fifth Avenue are gone, and fine old buildings are being callously demolished: 'These city planners and these boxes have killed all that. There isn't any roof line any more.' The new glass buildings rising overnight from gutted sites are for Tobey not an international style – they are 'international death'. Though he has been drawn toward America's human vitality, its picturesque folkways, and some of its landscape, Tobey has never been entirely at home here. On leaving an exhibition in Chicago which included Pollock and Rothko (whose painting he especially admires), his sharpest memory was of a work by Edward Hopper, whose factual poetry translated to him 'the loneliness and solitude that is in American psychology, and that thing talked more to me than all those other paintings... I have lived all over America except the South; ... actually lived these damned streets on Sunday where not even a cat is seen ... It's that kind of a life that can live without extensions. Isolationism. But not isolated by continents and water – isolated from spiritual currents...'

Among tensions in Tobey's thought other than that between the material and spiritual is the opposition of past to future. The two directions resemble each other: 'To rediscover the past is to move forward. There is no surcease when we constantly destroy what we have built. The future is carved with the implements we created before it was upon us. The past offers the art student different roads, all converging towards his present. Today's present appears different, more confusing; voices cry from all quarters. It used to be dangerous to know. Today it's dangerous not to know. What was close and established must now make room for newcomers. There is much groaning and some growls. Art, forever free,

Plate 6 *Broadway* 1936. Tempera.
26×19¾. The Metropolitan Museum
of Art, New York

seeks freedom from man's tyranny.'[25]

Tobey's 'philosophy' of art (if the use of the term can be permitted for an organic, rather than a systematized body of ideas) reflects his attitudes toward the past, present, and future, and also toward nontemporality. His experience had prepared him to respond with sympathy when, late in the forties, André Malraux hypnotized the reading world by dramatizing modern knowledge of art and its wide dissemination through museums, photographs and prints, art books, and technical advances. Tobey's art history began with the idealized figure painting and sculpture of the Renaissance – the style against which modernism was in revolt, but which Tobey has never totally discarded. Gradually his horizon expanded to include the leading masters of Eastern as well as Western art.[26] To wander through a museum with Tobey is to share in a succession of responses, warm acceptances, and instant dismissals. In principle, he does not avoid influence from any quarter: 'There is no such thing as a distinctly original artist. Every artist has his patron saints whether or not he is willing to acknowledge them. When an influence is strong enough, give in to it.'[27] But Tobey's painting seldom shows specific derivation. Pervading though it is, the influence of China and Japan is general, and thoroughly assimilated. His 'cubism' was his own from the beginning. Some of the religious paintings intentionally reflect medieval stained glass, architecture, or Italian and Byzantine frescoes and icons. Totem poles and other Northwest Indian artefacts are both a subject matter and a plastic influence. A collector of all sorts of primitive art, Tobey draws no line between a gallery of art and an ethnological museum.

Some of his most recognizable derivations are from Near Eastern, medieval, and Oriental calligraphy and ornament, and from those primitive styles having graphic signs compatible with twentieth-century form. A list of such instances, some confined to a single work, would include Egyptian picto-graphs, cuneiform, Coptic and Peruvian textiles, Australian bark painting, Arabic, Persian, and Hebrew script, and Celtic illumination. This list could be augmented with another from the contemporary environment of billboards, street signs, scientific symbols, punctuation and other graphic devices, unexpected effects in picture-magazine photographs, the end papers of old books, and an endless inventory of markings, patterns, and structures in nature. More revealing, perhaps, than to ferret out the scattered sources of Tobey's graphic language is to indicate the ideology that explains its diversity: 'When I was a young man, I never heard of Byzantine art . . . Now, above the horizon has come the beauty of Byzantine art – not only that, but the art the coloured people have, and the art of the Coptics, and all of the Orient and everything that has flooded the world.

'Now it seems to me that we are in a universalizing period . . . If we are to have world peace, we should have an understanding of all the idioms of beauty because the members of humanity who have created these idioms of beauty are going to be a part of us. And I would say that we are in a period when we are discovering and becoming acquainted with these idioms for the first time . . .'[28]

Tobey is moved by both constancy and change, and also by the nontemporalization – one could almost say 'spatialization' – of styles: a 'universal marshland, wherein lie forms of ancient ideas and cultures apparently unrelated to us but only waiting for time to reveal themselves upon the arc of our consciousness.'[29] He sees Gothic art, for example, exhausting itself 'in an electric light fixture in a café in the Far West.'[30]

The many oppositions of Tobey's thought – religion and science, Orient and Occident, spiritual and material, evolution and timelessness among them – bring about the same equilibrium that he seeks in his painting: 'It is a state of equilibrium which must be maintained if man is to move, to go forward.'[31]

THEMES AND SUBJECTS

by

William C. Seitz

Every artist's problem today is 'What will we do with the Human?'[1]

Tobey's subjects are drawn from the totality of his ideas, beliefs, and experiences, even though they sometimes must take form in variations of a single brush movement. He is deeply concerned with the universal themes of man, nature and God. Therefore, like many other modern painters who associate art with humanism, he has had to reconcile his movement toward abstractness with more than five millennia of figurative art. He has painted many self-portraits. One of his youthful ambitions, barely abandoned even today, was to become a figure painter or sculptor.[2] In portraits, sketches, caricatures, religious compositions, or street scenes he has represented almost every social group and type: saints, society women, vendors and workers, actors and entertainers, dancers, prostitutes, and skid-row bums. His interest is never satiric, nor that of the 'social realist,' but it can become abstract: 'Two men dressed in white jeans with white caps on their heads are climbing over a large sign of white letters . . . What is important is their white, and the white of their letters.'[3]

As a humanist, however, Tobey deplores the abstractness – aesthetic as well as technical and scientific – of modern life. Portraits are difficult to paint today, he says, 'because we do not believe in man.' With exhibitions as well as art schools in mind, he berates the 'abstract academy,' and paintings which are arresting but empty: 'We're getting so abstract that we are practically Arabs. The whole Arab world, outside of Persia, is design in the abstract sense. Figuration is taboo.' With these views, why did Tobey become a leader of the avant-garde? And why are Rothko, Lippold, and Mathieu among his favourite artists? The answer, which demonstrates how fully Tobey responds to the problems of his time, arises from his fourfold involvement with humanity, with nature, with the past, and with the future. The experimental temper projected him into new forms, as he has suggested, almost against his will. At one pole are his figure paintings; at the other are nonfigurative works: *New York* (Plate 45) and *The Voice of the Doll* (Plate 28) were painted the same year. Because of the need to reconcile this conflict work by work, Tobey's development was slow and dialectical: 'You see when I did all of these things nobody was doing them, and I had no support so I didn't know where I was, you see. And yet I had to do it, and I had a hard time, out of my love of figures, not to carry that along, because I like figures and I like people . . .'

While in Japan sitting on the floor of a room and looking over an intimate garden with flowers blooming and dragonflies hovering in space, I sensed that this small world almost under foot, shall I say, had a validity all its own . . . which must be realized and appreciated from its own level in space.[4]

. . . If it were not for his absorption in human problems Tobey's attitude toward nature would approach that of Taoism and Zen. He has painted animals, fish, birds, and insects, and recalls a question of his friend Teng Kuei, who asked, one day while they were looking at an aquarium in a restaurant window: 'Why do Western artists only paint a fish after it is dead?' He has painted gardens, trees, many kinds of landscape, dawn, dusk, and night. But Tobey's naturalism did not originate in Oriental influence; his tender feeling for natural states, birds, and animals began, as it will be shown, in childhood. But, even in the Oriental sense, Tobey is not a 'landscape painter.' As his comment on *Drift of Summer* (1942) emphasizes, he paints structures and processes: 'Above and floating free above matted grasses, delicate thread-like structures rise and float, wind-blown as the summer passes.'[5] Other images and titles relate to crystallization, drifting seeds or clouds, condensation, massing and dissolution. While painting he awaits the moment when (in the words of a Japanese friend) he can 'get out of the way,' and 'let nature take over.'[6]

The masterpiece of Tobey's nature paintings – a direct outcome of *Drift of Summer* and a prelude to the Meditative Series – is the great *Edge of August* (1953, page 23). The theme was in Tobey's mind for ten years before he could paint it successfully. Directly and without representation, as in music, this radical composition – 'something that could shift out of sight, away' – recreates a last essence of peace and warmth: '*Edge of August* is trying to express the thing that lies between two conditions of nature, summer and fall. It's trying to capture that transition and make it tangible. Make it sing. You might say that it's bringing the intangible into the tangible.'[7] The universe of the artist's consciousness is still permeated with delicate scents, pulsation, unnameable tactile sensations, and the murmur of movements audible only because of the silence around them. The iridescent field of minute calligraphy, modulating through the pale spectrum 'that one sees around the moon,' ends abruptly at the lower left – an area occupied in the later *Above the Earth V* (1956), by the quadrant of a sphere. The trembling cloud of writing is painted off the frame at the left, but at the right it fades into a dark void which represents, perhaps, the anxiety surrounding most moments of tranquility.

To anyone who has followed the pattern of Tobey's thinking and feeling, it will be evident that categories of subject must break down: Broadway is a river; cultures are separated by canals; a photograph of a crowd is a flower garden; a city is a crystal. As Gorky did, Tobey sees in visual metaphors. Because of this, and because Tobey is a symbolist, a series of intangible themes runs through his art that is independent of overt subject matter. *Light*, following its traditional symbolism, is associated with divinity, enlightenment, and spirituality. 'Turner is greater than the Impressionists,' in Tobey's mind, because 'he dissolved everything into light.'[8] Since 1920 Tobey has thought of light as structure. The Paris cafés of the twenties were 'foci for people who wanted light to see in the night. They wanted light to sit in, to look at their friends, and talk . . .' Another of these themes – 'operational,' so to speak – is *migration*: the wandering of microscopic life, electricity, spores and seeds, birds and animals; of human beings and their thoughts, artefacts, art and architecture; of religions and cultures. Movement lines can indicate change from any one of these levels to others, or from one compartment of existence to another. Viewed symbolically in Tobey's mind, the breakup of

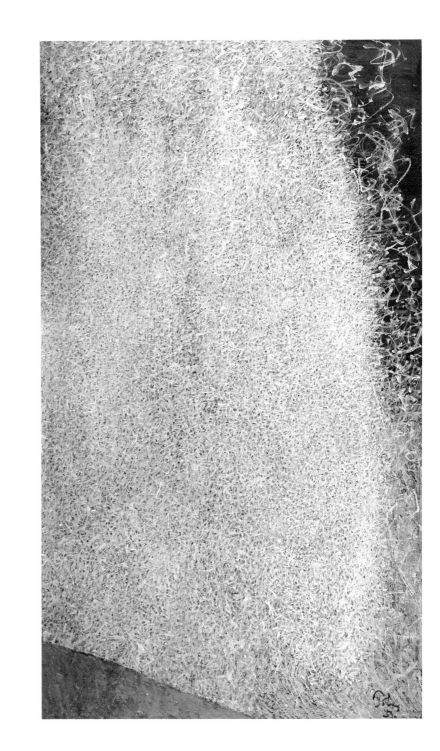

Plate 7 *Edge of August* 1953. Tempera. 48×28.
The Museum of Modern Art, New York, purchase

Renaissance perspective and illusionism in favour of multiple space and moving focus is a historical parallel to the gradual dissolution of barriers between egos, nations, and cultures. When the level of vision rises and its horizon expands, so does the ethical consciousness. *Space* is for Tobey, as for many modern artists, a theme as well as an illusion of painting; the space in which we live every day, the blanket of atmospheric space around the earth, and the 'inner space' conceived by the mind: 'My imagination, it would seem, has its own geography.'[9] *Scale* is also a theme: evident in the shift of magnitude from a crystal dish to a metropolis, or from a close-up to a telescopic view, and in the compression of encompassing concepts into tiny pictures. It is a question of the 'scale of relativity': 'I don't care if it's a picture eight feet high or eight inches high; to me it should have scale . . . If it doesn't have that, then it's a repetition of experiences that are the same.' In a similar sense, one can say that *unity* and *equilibrium* are subjects as well as conditions of Tobey's art.

In its essence, the movement of Tobey's mind is not simply migratory but anagogic, like that of medieval mysticism, from which it differs in drawing not from scholastic thought but from the complexity of modern experience. Perhaps more than any other modern artist – though one must compare Klee, Mondrian, Kandinsky, and Brancusi – Tobey has given form to mystical states, to worship. The texture, rhythm, and modes of formation of his *summa* are therefore at least as important as its content. Certain of his religious conceptions are represented; but more characteristically, experience is transmuted into form without an intermediary image. Transcendental human consciousness, it could be said, is Tobey's ultimate theme. Those pictures which convey it directly are his best answer to the coarse assertion that only the depiction of flesh is 'humanistic.' If man is a part of nature, Tobey says, 'a landscape can be humanistic . . . Can the human be seen in the abstract? Saint Francis is a vertical.

Humanism is not just figuration. The "return to the figure" does not make you a humanist. It may make you an anti-humanist.'

An artist must find his expression closely linked to his individual experience or else follow in the old grooves resulting in lifeless forms.[10]

. . . Tobey's art and ideas [went through a] long period of gestation and formation, and he was forty-five years old before their diverse elements began to coalesce. Before that time, though there are fine and even masterful pictures, his production is contradictory in style and uneven in quality. Erratic, but logical in retrospect, Tobey's path was a rigorous discipline as well as a self-conducted apprenticeship. The events that directed him were as varied as the paintings, many of them dispersed or destroyed, that punctuate his phases. Artists have two biographies: one made up of the same personal events as the lives of nonartists, and another contained in a different order of time – a ladder of reflection and illumination like that ascended by a philosopher or a mystic.[11] Tobey has always felt that the artist's role was 'to be a filter of life, so that other people could see what that condensation is.' His 'inner' biography, moreover, is of special interest because its expansion from isolation to internationalism, and from illustration to inspired abstraction, shows little resemblance to the pattern, varied though it is, by which Western artists are most often trained.

. . . A power to absorb and symbolize the discrepant realities of an entire period has been a sign of greatness in an artist from the time of Phidias to that of Cézanne and Picasso. Tobey's structures of lines, strokes, and signs have this kind of inclusiveness: they are seismographic records of the contemporary mind and sensibility as it responds to the delights, dangers, staggering challenges, and unprecedented potentialities of life in our time. There are of course significant aspects of human experience that find no place in his art, but it is amazing to comprehend the breadth of compass this profound painter has achieved. He has been consistently led to draw a greater diversity of meaning into the distilled sphere of his art. In a new temporal and geographic context, Tobey's aim is identical with that attributed by George Rowley to Confucianism and Taoism, the two modes of thought that lie behind Chinese painting: 'They both sought "inner reality" in a fusion of opposites.'[12] Followed to their universal meeting ground, many of the polarities that Rowley discovered in Oriental painting – spirit and matter, divine and human, personal and impersonal, man and nature, tradition and originality, expansion and contraction, delicacy and power, improvization and preparation – are also among those that make up Tobey's content and form.

Even in more specific characteristics, Tobey's equilibrium derives from a ying-yang of contradictions. In the geography of ideas, he came from nowhere. His speech, mannerisms, and many of his tastes are Midwestern. Much of his subject matter is as Yankee, in its own way, as that of Sheeler, Hopper, or Curry. He is the founding master of the 'Northwest School' of painting. Yet at the same time Tobey may well be the most internationally minded painter of importance in the history of art. What could better illustrate his increasing internationalism than the evolution of his idea of line and brush? It began with the ornamental embellishments of Harrison Fisher and other cover-girl specialists, progressed to *Jugendstil* and the bravura of Sargent and Sorolla, expanded to include Hals, and finally came to encompass most of the world's calligraphic art, and great Eastern masters like Liang K'ai and Sesshu. What an unprecedented fusion of perspectives!

Tobey is a humanist, a traditionalist, a lover of the body as a subject and humanity as a theme. Nevertheless – under the influence of modern existence rather than modern art – he was led to fragment, obscure, and ultimately to dematerialize the human form and image entirely, in search of a valid expression of the human spirit. Belatedly but by sheer awareness of modern life, he found himself projected to the apex of contemporary abstract style.

Art is the centre of Tobey's activity. Like facets of the visible environment, therefore, his ethical, philosophical, and religious convictions should perhaps be regarded only as components and sources. Yet it is hard to ignore Tobey the social critic, religious reformer, or even the prophet. His adoption of free brush as a means was not a technical coup but a philosophical conclusion. Long before the world was polarized into two nuclear arsenals, Tobey knew that the hiatus between East and West should be closed. Contracting the globe to eye-range, he foretold and led the aesthetic counter-rotation of the world which is now bringing into balance forces that have indeed met like 'long-lost lovers.'

In Tobey's philosophy there is no break between aesthetic and political imperatives: the ego must soften and open; baneful divisions must be bridged; misunderstandings must be resolved. If society is to avoid a catastrophe, the consciousness of man must be universalized. Equilibrium is as necessary in life as in painting. The world must become one. For Tobey one great need, if this fulfilment is to be realized, is the reconciliation of science with religion.

These two paths toward truth, one ancient and the other modern, do not yet meet. Is it possible that they can be reconciled, if at all, only through art?

Plate 8 *E Pluribus Unum* 1942. Tempera. $19\frac{3}{4} \times 27\frac{1}{4}$. The Seattle Art Museum, gift of Mrs Thomas D. Stimson, 43.33

LOOKING AT TOBEY'S PICTURES

by

Joshua C. Taylor

For the past forty years the paintings of Mark Tobey have been a special and glowing ingredient in the broad cross section of experiences we associate with American art. His very personal expression has sometimes intermingled with popular movements and theories but has never lost its identity. A painting by Tobey has always provided a view into a private world of vision and spirit rather than an invitation to a critical world of schools and trends. With extraordinary persistence he has kept his sights on a beatific goal, seeing painting as a means for breaking down the false limits of materiality that bind the spirit to a profitless world. Yet he has been very much a part of the urban culture of our time, finding creative excitement in the entangling activity and threatening visual chaos of the modern city as well as in the more tranquil countryside. Nature for Tobey is to be found in man, and man finds his true being in spirit. Without sermonizing or lapsing into abstruse symbols, Tobey's painting, with its demanding intricacies and its ecstatic intensity, provides a way to the spirit, to that point at which aesthetic refinement becomes identical with spiritual release. His luminous world belongs to all men. It is in gratitude for his great personal contribution through art that this exhibition is presented.

This exhibition is not retrospective in the usual sense of that term. It is not, that is, an effort to spread out the life of the artist on the walls of a gallery to be walked past in a casual hour. Tobey's work lends itself very poorly to this kind of treatment. To be sure, in his long career he has passed through many changes in painterly thought and method, and with some effort these can be neatly labelled and summarized. But Tobey's paintings do not reveal themselves most readily when looked upon as links in a chain; from his early years each work has demanded a kind of individual attention that serves to cut off its connection to a before or an after. His art is not to be summed up in a glance but opens itself only to patience and time. Time is possibly the clue: not time to be counted in minutes or hours but time to be spent in a continuing, unquestioning journey of sense and mind.

In the clock-punctuated life we lead, it is sometimes difficult to remember – although Henri

Joshua C. Taylor was Director of the National Collection of Fine Arts, Washington, DC. This essay, originally untitled, is from the catalogue of the exhibition at the National Collection of Fine Arts in 1974 'Tribute to Mark Tobey'.

Bergson made much of the fact many years ago – that time was not invented by clocks. For most, time usually comes to mean measure, measure comes to signify limitation, and, given its limitation, time becomes something we rarely have. But Tobey demands that for the moment we suspend our habit of telling time to savour the experiences the passage of time provides, to discover the complexity and expansiveness of a living world in which time has neither beginning nor ending.

Over the years Tobey has developed many ways to stop our delimiting clocks and awaken us to a more extensible world. From the beginning he persisted in seeing the small revealing part instead of squinting at the whole. His view of the Broadway of 1936 is bewildering because he refuses to allow anything to be shut out. Noise, lights, and people ply the senses with so complex an entanglement that the street itself is lost in the continuous discovery of particular instances. Neither tidy forms nor isolated things break the rather frantic process of looking. This is true as well in his *E Pluribus Unum* (page 26), in which there are simply too many individual people to make a judgement about man in general. The oneness is not a visual homogeneity but a pervading energy, everywhere apparent and everywhere different. Contrary to the tradition of formal idealism in art, in which the likeness of man approaches its spiritual source to the degree it subordinates individual characteristics, Tobey's chattering populace is a nagging cluster of unresolvable individuals, neither especially beautiful nor markedly grotesque, linked only by a shared vitality. They catch the eye as they appear and disappear in the crowd, looming large or remaining almost unidentifiable but *there*, and a feeling that someone else may be discovered, who was not there before, haunts the scene. One has to go back and look again.

It is a source of some pathos that, for all the exuberance of human vitality in a painting like *E Pluribus Unum* or, even more, in *Electric Night* no one seems to be talking to anyone else. Pathetic little figures emerge from the shiny entanglement of lines which seem to resist the very energies that produce them. There is an evident discrepancy between the vitality of the whole and that sensed by the individual, as if the restless energy were yet to be tapped as a source of human strength.

This process of looking at a crowd, hovering on the border between generalized energy and individual human pathos, is not so very different from the way that Tobey demands we see his paintings that display no figures at all. All are basically contemplation pieces that afford the mind an extraordinary range of both action and rumination. The persuasive rhythms, which demand our participation and yet are far from muscular, carry the burden of present time, while the hints of specific figures or faces or preoccupying knotlike formulations prod the memory to add an unending series of images and thoughts to what might otherwise be simply a rhythmic gesture.

Tobey took great care in the 1940s to ensure that the full mind enter into his linear play, quite probably fearing the superficiality of a too easy abstraction. He need not have feared, because as he depended less and less on his memory-tripping figures, his line took on a new content of its own. For Tobey, line seems always to have been more energy than matter, a path more than a boundary. When, in 1935, he became fascinated with the continuous, entangling line, he discovered for himself something that he might have found in Lipps's theories of empathy as understood earlier in the century, or in his own Oriental calligraphic studies. Usually Tobey's interest in Chinese calligraphy is cited as a major element in the development of his mature work, and it might well be. It should be noted, however, that his thrusts and curves use few actual Chinese strokes, and that there was a long period between Tobey's original interest in Chinese brush technique and his first use of the calligraphic line. Quite evidently it had to be made his own, allied with personal content, and not assumed as a borrowed method. Yet this in itself is not outside the Chinese tradition. While much artistic formation in the West is based on proportion and external measure, the goal of Chinese training was to re-capture the spiritual vitality that was evident in the brush-work of the great masters of calligraphy, handing on less an external mark of style than an internal continuity of spirit. Art was a continuous re-experiencing, a re-creation. The 'spirit of the brush,' as the Chinese masters called the almost magical identity between brush stroke and an impersonal, vital spirit, was rekindled by Tobey in his own world of lights and noise and telephone wires. What had once been simple rhythms became, under the power of the brush, a varied cast of expressive agents, some shy, some aggressive, and some winningly lyrical.

Furthermore, while our own physical actions are performed one at a time, movements sensed visually can coexist, retreating and overlapping, struggling for dominance like the evasive subjects of a complex fugue. Space, as well as time, is continuously variable in Tobey. Although he may pretend to set forth a systematic organization in depth, as in *New York Tablet*, it is a Pirandello-like conceit because some-where between the top plane and the last we lose our point of reference and slip into the fluctuating relationship that is stable only when no questions are asked. The standpoint of the viewer, in other words, is effectively dissolved, leaving him free to wander on a long trip of discovery.

And what is discovered? It would be tempting to say the self, or the self of the artist. Or possibly we could say that the artist allows us to sense creativity by joining him in his work. But none of these seems right. Certainly a concept of self was early purged from Tobey's paintings. While every stroke is evident and obviously is a gesture of his hand, it seems to obey the laws of some unspoken ritual rather than to respond to personal expression. We follow each line into the multidimensional maze, but there is little to encourage us to suppose that we have created it, or to be conscious of the artist who did. The bold bravura strokes of Sargent or Boldini invite us to share in the evident confidence and self-satisfaction of the artist; Tobey's brush strokes allow for no such expansive self-congratulation. Without seeming organic in the way of Arp or Gorky, Tobey's lines and forms have a busy life of their own, often chastely engaged in a kind of irresistible flocking. We are free to join them if we wish, recognizing that to join is to surrender to a kind of cosmic busyness in which to be active is to be at peace. It is a cosmos for contemplation, yet, since it is built out of minute awareness of the particularities of sight and touch and sound, it does not separate itself from our mundane environment: it transforms it. Light becomes alive and the world ticks with a new rhythm.

But to generalize about Tobey is to betray him. There is no single Tobey form or pattern; there is, instead, the expression of inexhaustible delight in exploration and discovery that finds its way through many paths and formulations. Each painting is a sepa-rate activity, requiring patience and attention in its own way. Yet the rewards are consistent, and we recognize with pleasure the special world to which Tobey has admitted us.

Plate 9 *Aerial Centers* Collection Arthur Lyon and Martine Dahl

Plate 10 *Burst of Spring* 1964. Tempera. 50½×32.
Private Collection

THE FRAGRANCE OF SPIRITUALITY

An Appreciation

by

Arthur Lyon Dahl

Art has long been one of the highest expressions of human culture, and particularly of its religious and spiritual dimensions. The cave paintings of early man, the temples and tombs of the Egyptians, Greeks, Hindus and Buddhists, the churches, cathedrals and mosques of more modern times, are so often the greatest examples of a culture's artistic heritage, and still communicate their spirit to us today. Yet what survives is generally the reflection of a mature culture; there is seldom any trace of those creative attempts in periods of rapid cultural change and in particular in the early days of a new religious age to break free from the confines of a traditional heritage and to seek fresh means of expression for the new beliefs.

Arthur Lyon Dahl owns several paintings by Mark Tobey and has given numerous lectures on the artist. He is an active member of the Bahá'í Faith, as an Auxiliary Board Member in New Caledonia, where he was until recently Regional Ecological Advisor to the South Pacific Commission. A version of this essay was originally published in The Bahá'í World, *1976-9, Vol. XVII.*

Mark Tobey lived and worked in what will probably be judged by history to be one of those periods of social and cultural transition. As one of the first Bahá'ís to achieve world recognition for his artistic accomplishments, especially for the creativity with which he sought to express the intangible and spiritual in human experience, it is appropriate to examine his contribution to art, with particular reference to the influence of the Bahá'í Faith.

Mark Tobey's development as a painter involved a slow maturation marked by many stages of creative synthesis and discovery as he explored new concepts and drew on new experiences. His rural childhood and almost complete lack of formal training isolated him from the customary European artistic heritage. Early success as a portraitist demonstrated his innate talent, and his evolution from figurative through symbolic to abstract forms of expression resulted more from his intense inner motivation and his cumulative life experiences than from any attempt to follow the trends of modern art. Since he was neither geographically nor emotionally in the mainstream of cultural fashion, his accomplishments were slow to be generally recognized, particularly in his own country where, in the artistic capital New York, it was inconceivable that an outsider could indeed be ahead of its own avant-garde. A few perceptive individuals supported his efforts, but the general reaction was one of vague interest, indifference or worse. Tobey's first real acclaim came at an age when most people are ready for retirement. From the late 1950s, the many awards and exhibitions demonstrated the growing recognition of his accomplishments and the widespread acknowledgement that he was probably America's greatest living artist.[1] Yet this recognition failed to divert him from his dedication to art. He resented the demands of fame which distracted him from his painting, and indeed continued to produce major works and to explore new forms of expression nearly to the end of his life.

He also struggled with the often difficult choices involved in balancing his responsibility to his art and his direct service to the Bahá'í Faith, sometimes abandoning his painting for months at a time to undertake Bahá'í activities. Yet Bahá'u'lláh wrote: 'The possessors of sciences and arts have a great right among the people of the world',[2] and 'Abdu'l-Bahá has added: '. . . when the studying of art is with the intention of obeying the command of God this study will certainly be done easily and great progress will soon be made therein; and when others discover this fragrance of spirituality in the action itself, this same will cause their awakening.'[3]

It is at this level that the Bahá'í Faith has had the most profound and pervasive impact on Tobey's paintings. His dedication to art was reinforced by his beliefs. Indeed, his entire approach to art was conditioned by this potent combination. He wrote: 'This universal Cause of Bahá'u'lláh which brings the fruition of man's development, challenges him and attracts him to see the light of this day as the unity of all life; dislodges him from a great deal of automatic and environmental inheritance: seeks to create in him a vision which is absolutely necessary for his existence. The teachings of Bahá'u'lláh are themselves the

light with which we can see how to move forward on the road of evolution.'[4]

Tobey was dislodged from his surrounding artistic inheritance by his discovery of the Bahá'í Faith, and launched a new direction in the evolution of art. For him, 'my whole idea of my painting is experiencing my life in paint.'[5] and this of course included the new spirit he had found, a spirit which he felt had died out of the art world.[6] 'To me an artist is one who . . . portrays the spirit of man in whatever condition that spirit may be. We can't expect too much of him when the rest is negligent of spiritual values such as today.'[7] He spent his life in a quest for means of expressing this new spirit, a spirit reflected not only in his Faith but also in the dramatic changes being brought about by science in society. 'At a time when experimentation expresses itself in all forms of life, search becomes the only valid expression of the spirit . . .'[8] 'I am accused often of too much experimentation, but what else should I do when all other factors of man are in the same condition? Shall any member of the body live independently of the rest? I thrust forward into space as science and the rest do. My activity is the same, therefore my end will be similar. The gods of the past are as dead today as they were when Christianity overcame the Pagan world. The time is similar, only the arena is the whole world.'[9] He tried to balance his external and internal experiences: 'One is so surrounded by the scientific naturally one reflects it, but one needs (I mean the artist now) the religious side. One might say the scientific aspect interests the mind, the religious side frees the heart. All are interesting.'[10] Yet this was not basically a conscious process, but a reflection of the whole man. 'The development of my work has been I feel more subconscious than conscious. I do not work by intellectual deductions. My work is a kind of self-contained contemplation.'[11]

The Bahá'í Faith also gave Tobey a world view, an openness to the diversity of human experience both in the subjects he depicted and in the cultural traditions which he searched for techniques and inspiration. His openness to Oriental art and his synthesis of elements of that art into his own were some of the early creative achievements underlying his later development, leading some critics to consider this the fundamental aspect of his art. To this he responded: 'as to the content of my own work, well, in spite of the comments regarding my interest in Zen, it has never been as deep as my interest in the Bahá'í Faith.'[12] He was particularly attracted to cultural periods where the expression of faith or inner spiritual states was important, not only in Oriental art but also in Christian art (Byzantine and medieval) and that of the American Indians, and he frequently drew on themes from such art in his own work.

There is also in the Bahá'í Writings a new perspective on the history of man, the evolution of human society, and the particular point at which we find ourselves today, and this too helped Tobey to place his own accomplishment. 'New seeds are no doubt being sown which mean new civilizations and, let us hope, cultures too. If I do anything important in painting some age will bring it forth and understand. One naturally looks forward to the time when absolutes will reign no more and all art will be seen as valid . . . Shall we, as we view the increasingly darkening sky, not hope for a Byzantium, some spot to keep alight the cultural values? For what else shall we live?'[13]

It is almost impossible to summarize Mark Tobey's accomplishments in art. He has treated such a wide range of subjects in an incredible diversity of styles and media that for every generality there are immediately exceptions. Most of his paintings are relatively small, intended for an intimate rapport with the viewer. Recognizable figures or forms become less and less evident as his art evolved, yet there is still a strong feeling of 'representation' in the majority of his paintings. He was capable of selecting the most visually significant elements of a scene and concen-

trating them onto the surface in a way that would re-create in the viewer a more complete experience. It might be the colour and movement of blades of grass in a field, the flash of lights in night traffic, or stars and mists in an evening sky. He would search out striking visual impressions and natural beauty of every kind, the surface of a squashed tin can, radio beacons, old walls of buildings, the veins of a leaf, often noting similarities between disparate elements in a leap of creative recognition.

After an experience imagining himself to be a fly moving around a room, he was able to develop a kind of multiple space, a personal version of cubism, in which the viewer has no fixed perspective, but finds that his eyes wander through the painting as though viewing a three-dimensional object from many angles.

In his explorations of Oriental art, he learned the subtleties of expression of which the brush is capable in calligraphy, the art developed from Oriental writing in both the Far East and in the Arabic and Persian cultures associated with the early Bahá'ís. This discovery gave him freedom of form in artistic expression, and he first applied it to express what especially interested him in the life of cities, 'the lights, the electric cables of the trolleys, the human streams directed by, through and round prescribed limits.'[14] This was the beginning of his 'white writing' and of a concentration on the many characteristics of light which developed into a larger symbolism. 'White lines in movement symbolize light as a unifying idea which flows through the compartmented units of life bringing a dynamic to men's minds, ever expanding their energies toward a larger relativity.'[15] He could capture certain qualities of light, soft moonlight or the bright lights of a carnival, and would often use this to convey a larger message. It is interesting to note the parallel with the frequent symbolic use of light for spirit in the Bahá'í Writings.

Tobey also developed the technical means for

Plate 11 *The Red Tree of the Martyr* 1940. Tempera. $9\frac{1}{2} \times 13\frac{1}{2}$. Collection Arthur Lyon and Martine Dahl

expressing space, energy and motion. His paintings can represent an empty, infinite depth as in *Void*, or burst with explosive energy as in *New Genesis*, a work that may well express the creative force of the new religious impulse. They often contain multiple layers of elements, charged with movement or submerged in a placid calm.

With this new artistic vocabulary at his disposal, Tobey was able to create, on his two-dimensional surface, images communicating normally non-visual concepts and even emotions. In *Edge of August* (page 23), for instance, the shimmering heat and saturated greenish light of summer fade out into a nearly empty autumn in a potent depiction of the changing seasons. '*Edge of August* is trying to express the thing that lies between two conditions of nature, summer and fall. It's trying to capture that transition and make it tangible. Make it sing. You might say that it's bringing the intangible into the tangible.'[16] *Remote Field* (1944, Plate 49) conveys the emptiness and desolation of war, while a lighter touch is evident in such pictures as *Calligraphic Still Life No. 3* (Plate 65), a humorous play on normal concepts of perspective.

He explained his lack of a regular progression in his work in a 1955 letter. 'Over the past 15 years, my approach to painting has varied, sometimes being dependent on brush-work, sometimes on lines, dynamic white strokes in geometric space. I have never tried to pursue a particular style in my work. For me, the road has been a zigzag into and out of old civilizations, seeking new horizons through meditation and contemplation. My sources of inspiration have gone from those of my native Middle West to those of microscopic worlds. I have discovered many a universe on paving stones and tree barks. I know very little about what is generally called "abstract" painting. Pure abstraction would mean a type of painting completely unrelated to life, which is unacceptable to me. I have sought to make my painting "whole" but to attain this I have used a whirling mass. I take up no definite position. Maybe this explains

someone's remark while looking at one of my paintings: "Where is the center?" '[17]

Since there were no precedents for him to follow, the creation of a successful painting was often a matter of trial and error under appropriately-creative conditions, and Tobey's letters often refer to many paintings wiped off or discarded as failures, and to periods when conditions were not right for advancing his work. 'A State of Mind is the first preparation and from this the action proceeds. *Peace of Mind* is another ideal, perhaps the ideal state to be sought for in the painting and certainly preparatory to the act.'[18] 'What matters most is keeping the eyes open for experience in new directions. Perhaps the Orient is inclusive of what we term the accidental. The accidental can lead one back toward the conscious again if accepted and used; it can lead to art.'[19]

A key to appreciating Mark Tobey's painting is a recognition of the effort he expected on the part of the viewer. He described his own experience in learning how to approach Oriental art: 'When I resided at the Zen monastery I was given a sumi-ink painting of a large free brush circle to meditate upon. What was it? Day after day I would look at it. Was it selflessness? Was it the Universe – where I could lose my identity? Perhaps I didn't see its aesthetic and missed the fine points of the brush which to a trained Oriental eye would reveal much about the character of the man who painted it. But after my visit I found I had new eyes and that which seemed of little importance became magnified in words, and considerations not based on my former vision.'[20] For him, understanding art meant exchanging human experiences: '. . . unless the person is willing to go through some of the actual experiences of the living artist and of those whose paintings are left behind in art museums all over the world as living symbols of their own experience, they remain as persons un-initiated.'[21] But he knew that the result could be highly enriching. 'The old Chinese used to say: "It is better to feel a painting than to look at it." So much today is only to look at. It is one thing to paint a picture and another to experience it: in attempting to find on what level one accepts this experience, one discovers what one sees and on what level the discovery takes place. Christopher Columbus left in search of one world and discovered another.'[22] Indeed, Tobey's friends and critics have often likened his paintings to the more emotional arts of poetry and music: 'Like poetry and music, his pictures have the time element, they unfold their contents gradually. With an active imagination they have to be approached, read, and their symbols interpreted. They reveal their tenor if one listens with the inner ear, "the ear of the heart," as Jean Paul calls it.'[23]

In my view, the most fundamentally significant of Mark Tobey's artistic accomplishments, underlying and indeed motivating much of his technical development, is his depiction of the spiritual dimension of man. It was only natural that he should express his Bahá'í experiences and emotions both explicitly and implicitly in his paintings, and during the long development of his artistic career he returned again and again to Bahá'í themes.

In *Conflict of the Satanic and Celestial Egos* (1918, Plate 18), painted shortly after he became a Bahá'í, he uses the artistic language of William Blake and Michelangelo to convey the struggle between man's physical and spiritual natures. As in the past, human forms are used to represent spiritual realities.

The 1930s, when he was making the major breakthroughs in his artistic development, saw a number of explicitly Bahá'í works produced. *Rising Orb* (1935) symbolically depicts the coming of a new Revelation. 'When we wake up and see the inner horizon light rising, then we see beyond the horizon [and] break the mould of men's minds with the spirit of truth. Then there will be greater relativity than before. This light will burn away the mist of life and will become very, very great.'[24] *The Seekers*, probably done in this period although dated 1950, shows nine figures gathered on either side of a fountain of flowing waters, while another figure looks on.

The martyrdoms which so marked the early history of the Bahá'í Faith provided a recurring subject for Tobey, even though, as he put it, 'I know that martyr subjects aren't popular . . .'[25] *Day of the Martyr* (1942, Plate 43) captures in its enclosed spaces, sombre reddish coloration and restrained figures, the anguish of oppression yet spiritual calm that must have surrounded the martyrs and their families. *The Red Tree of the Martyr* (1940, page 35), long one of Tobey's favourites, communicates the reverence and respect that the Bahá'ís feel for those who have given their lives for their Faith. 'It has the same inner spirit as the *Emerald Hill* (see below) but clearer – in beautiful dark warm reds . . . The rise of the grey wall behind is beautiful. Two Bahá'ís bow on either side. It is certainly expressive of the beauty of the Bahá'í Religion . . .'[26]

A similar historical foundation, but viewed in a different spirit, can be found in *The New Day* (1945?, Plate 39), in which scattered architectural elements and figures in nineteenth century Persian dress are enmeshed in a white writing based on Persian calligraphic motifs. Since Tobey has said that 'multiple space bounded by involved white lines symbolize higher states of consciousness, or dimensions spoken of in the Father's Kingdom,'[27] the white writing may represent the enveloping power of the Word of God as brought in the Bahá'í Revelation, while the scenes seem derived from *The Dawn-Breakers* (Nabíl's Narrative). The result concentrates the spirit of the early years of the Bahá'í Faith. *The Retreat of the Friend* (1947) seems similarly based on events associated with the early history of the Faith. Even in a less representational work like *Extensions from Baghdád* (1944), the spirit of Bahá'u'lláh's declaration in Baghdád is suggested in the 'fragments of the East, elements which writhe and coil, drawn into the western zones and evoking, for eternity, the unity of the human spirit.'[28]

A broader scope, that of the cultural development of mankind that comes with religious revelation, is condensed into *Arena of Civilization* (1947, Plate 40). 'The idea of layers of cultures or strata of civilizations existed from the moment of the picture's conception: this idea being that such layers break up and are disclosed so that the next layer can expand. This painting is a kind of miniature and for this reason is connected with the art of the Near East, but the subject uses material of both the east and the west...

'The draped forms of the East symbolize the spirit of Bahá'í which I believe to be the religion of our time and of the future, even if it is little known at the moment...

'The upper part of the painting symbolizes the new and higher forces of our age, those which we call modern; for this reason they are less formed but will take shape in the course of growth. These symbols do not only refer to the efficient machines of our modern age, but also to the spiritual and mental concepts connected with material progress. "Everything becomes evident by degrees"('Abdu'l-Bahá). It is the same with civilizations, and I personally think that man always ends up experimenting with truth. In Bahá'í the stress on "the unity of human beings" is something new, it is even the crux of the matter if we are to have peace. This is an age of new communications which necessitate a fresh kind of perspective or a new kind of eye with which to see. And so I have composed this picture from the richly loaded Writings of Bahá'u'lláh and His son 'Abdu'l-Bahá.'[29]

The Bahá'í view of the dangers of material civilization carried to excess is graphically depicted in *Void Devouring the Gadget Era* (1942, Plate 35), in what might be termed a spiritual interpretation of the effects of war. It represents an interesting development of Tobey's earlier paintings of the forms associated with modern material society.

In a more positive vein, *Concourse* (1943, Plate 42) symbolically depicts the 'army of light', the rank upon rank of heavenly souls marshalled by the saints and prophets of bygone ages, waiting to come to the aid of those who arise to serve the Bahá'í Cause. An even more joyful and harmonious heavenly celebration is captured in the warm colours and active brush-strokes of *Celestial Concert* (1954).

The subdued coloration of *The Emerald Hill of Faithfulness* (1952) reinforces the calm strength of the clustered forms seemingly anchored in place and bowed but not broken, set on a vast plain under an energy-charged sky. The faithful appear even more solidly placed than the green hill on the horizon in the distance.

As Tobey's work evolved, the non-figurative and non-symbolic elements in his art tended to increase, but many of his works continued to reflect Bahá'í themes in a more abstract form. The four scenes of *New World Dimensions I, II, III* and *IV* (1954, Plate 58), with their strong composition and harmonious colours, suggest states of society in a new world brought to fruition by the observance of the Divine teachings for today. They radiate a dynamic peace in which the human forms and their surroundings are dimly perceived, as becomes our images of the future society.

One of the most difficult subjects for a painter would seem to be prayer and meditation, yet even here Mark Tobey has succeeded in capturing a profound sense of a spiritual state, particularly in his *Meditative Series* of 1954, of which William Seitz has said: 'Visual prayers, these small, profound communions with God, nature, and the self transcribe the *activity*, as distinct from the subject matter, of meditation.'[30] Of *Meditative Series VIII* (Plate 54), Tobey said it 'can suggest so much – cosmic or just minute forces of nature.'[31] 'I try to make of each picture a world in itself, and perhaps this one seems uninteresting however much one looks at the variations in the relations of lines and in the accents of touch which I have used in the centre. A much vaster world can be found here than would appear at first glance. The use of many entwining rhythms indicates

Plate 12 *Lovers of Light* 1960. Tempera. $4\frac{3}{4} \times 6\frac{3}{4}$. Collection Arthur Lyon and Martine Dahl

my search for height and depth. One must search while one is contemplating or else there will be no reward.'[32] In the exquisite *Lovers of Light* (1960, page 39), painted when Tobey was 70 years old, the 'white writing' with which he has depicted both physical and spiritual light is refined to a crystalline delicacy and clarity, while being condensed into an unbelievably small space (the painting measures $4\frac{3}{4} \times 6\frac{3}{4}$ in.). The technical perfection of the extremely fine brush-work creates a complex of interconnected space and line that absorbs the viewer into an intimate spiritual communion.

It was only natural that Tobey's interest in spiritual subjects would go beyond the explicitly Bahá'í to draw on the great periods of spiritual expression in earlier cultures. He once wrote: 'I wouldn't mind revisiting the old beauties of Europe although my tendencies tend toward the Orient, or if in Europe, to the medieval where the two strains and attitudes meet in the abstraction of the human and divine ideas,'[33] and referring to a 12th-century sculpture, 'somewhere in this spirit I'd like to find an art which would represent the age to come...'[34] He frequently painted Christian and Biblical subjects such as the Last Supper, Adam and Eve, Jacob and the angel, or the dormition of the Virgin, drawing often on Byzantine or Gothic sources. He said with reference to one such painting: 'I have used some of the identical forms in improvization similar to musicians using a motif by earlier or contemporary musicians. I did not have any specific painting in mind, rather more or less the feeling of these paintings upon and into which I built a modern complex structure.'[35] Tobey's experience here would seem to parallel that of many Bahá'ís; his new Faith clarified and purified his understanding of the spiritual realities of earlier religious traditions as expressed in his own field of art.

Even beyond the obviously religious themes in Tobey's work, almost everything that he has done can be seen as an expression of the joy of discovering the beauties and attributes of God reflected visually as well as spiritually in the entire creation, a theme emphasized in his article from 1935, 'One Spirit' (see p.44).

It is generally agreed that Mark Tobey was a unique figure in contemporary art, standing aloof from yet often pioneering in the trends and directions of twentieth-century painting. The distinctive character of his work is obviously due not only to his innate talent and sensitivity, but also to his experience of the Bahá'í Faith, which provided him with a philosophical basis and approach totally different from that of his contemporaries. Indeed, even his move towards abstraction came from a different motivation, the search for an artistic language capable of expressing the spiritual and intangible.

He knew that only time could decide how his life and work related to history and human society, and how much influence the Bahá'í Faith exercised on his painting. 'I can only say that it has brought a tremendous impulse to me which I have tried to use without propaganda...'[36] He believed there would never be a 'Bahá'í art', but rather an evolution towards an acceptance of all art and a universality of expression. 'Of course we talk about international styles today, but I think later on we'll talk about universal styles... the future of the world must be this realization of its oneness, which is the basic teaching as I understand it in the Bahá'í Faith, and from that oneness will naturally develop a new spirit in art, because that's what it is. It's a spirit and it's not new words and it's not new ideas only. It's a different spirit. And that spirit of oneness will be reflected through painting.'[37] Mark Tobey pioneered the expression of that oneness and thus endowed his work with the 'fragrance of spirituality'.

TWO ESSAYS

by

Mark Tobey

Art and Community

In talking of Art to the man in the street, he says – 'It's beyond me. I can't even draw a straight line!' Expressions similar to these may be heard in communities of any size, whether small or large. Most people who work all day are under the impression that they haven't got time to consider such matters or even if they wanted to it's too late to begin.

In countries like America where the paths to culture are more consciously organized through lectures and reading, we find great activity about art, but few artists! In their mad rush to obtain culture in the same way they might buy a coat, they startle the artist and frighten him into the woods from their overemphasis on the mental side. The 'pigeon hole' process will give people many facts but unless the person is willing to go through some of the actual experiences of the living artist and of those whose paintings are left behind in the art museums all over the world as living symbols of their own experience, they remain as persons uninitiated. A great many people I am sure are earnest in their desire to contact art at first hand, but due to existing educational methods they are more often checked than liberated

along the line of their own impulse. Art clubs, art societies and art schools mostly form a barrier to the native contact. An extensive course in the history of painting may give one a magnificent scholastic approach, but more often leaves him with his eyes unopened, while his mouth parrots names, dates and what art critics and art authorities have had to say about the composition, colour, form and other elements of great paintings.

From my own experience, I have found far too many who have attended art schools and often a four-year course, have gone into the world and found themselves forced into any occupation except the one relating to their extensive training. Something must be sadly lacking when such an approach is so defeating. I would say it is mostly due to what might be called – 'progressive classes' – starting drawing from casts, then from life – painting from the nude with special classes in composition.

Secondly, and probably more important, it is the faraway goal of what one has to become before one's own elements can be accepted.

I am not trying to say that art is simple or that the

Plate 13 *Carnival* 1954. Tempera. $12\frac{1}{2} \times 7\frac{1}{4}$.
Collection Joyce Lyon Dahl

process of becoming an artist, a matter of hit or miss. But I do feel that the psychological factor in art education has been sadly neglected. That anyone is considered to be devoid of the creative faculty until a long prescribed course of study has been gone through, is like saying a tree is only a tree when it has reached maturity. The potentialities of art appreciation and creation are present in some degree in almost every child and when the right approach is made to liberate the adult from the mass hung on him or her by using educational methods, we still find that element alive and greatly appreciating any moments of release to be found in a direct approach.

Most of us in life are held back from doing the things we want to do by the structure of taboos generated by public opinion – approbation of friends or the fear of displeasing in more ways than one. The adult, in beginning to satisfy a long delayed desire in any field, should seek to become conscious as quickly as possible of the price to be paid for independence. For all things which separate us in consciousness from mass ideas, are more or less painful and the price of spiritual exertion over habits of long standing, equally so. If one could pick the state of self-consciousness and shyness to pieces, one would find that we live in quite as dark a world of taboos as the civilized man considers the savage to be in.

As it is easier as we grow older to throw aside curiosity and bury our own reactions in mass opinions, so it is to discard the creative impulse into the realms of dreams and what might have been.

All human beings are responsible to each other and the lack of this consciousness creates within communities restrictions and differences, for which the community as a whole pays the price of less expansion. Society as a whole has shut the door to the artist and creative person because they have individually and collectively shut the door to their own creative sides. Feeling people are too difficult and demand too much individual thought and time for the routine of their factual existence. When people of any community learn that art may become a functional part of their life they will find more life and not only that but a new eye and a new ear – and the artist will step down from his ivory tower only too glad to become a part of the whole again and both will come to see these and similar activities as the manifestations of a higher state of human consciousness – the vision of the whole.

The One Spirit

When we attempt to contemplate the *One Spirit* we come to an abstraction unknowable in any manner akin to our three-dimensional state of being or existence. So we look to its manifestations, numberless pluralities of its rich reflections, its valleys of grandeur, the powers of its exuberance as forms flow from forms – expressing this same richness in massive rocks or opening to us in some delicate blossom, as though an eye of extreme beauty had opened, fresh in its birth from harder and less reflecting substances but fed and related to them by some secret stream of life.

As we walk through these conditions, we can well ask ourselves (and especially in these days), are we related to these other manifestations, or do we feel ourselves independent, as though we were creatures of finer substances and therefore above – superior to and free from them?

In this age of seeming mastery over the forces of nature we appear as kings of *magic power*, as we view our rise into the air, finding ourselves everywhere surrounded by numberless slaves of nature contributing to our comfort and pleasure, apparently almost lifeless objects – yet functioning for our advantage, helping us to conquer space, enabling us to break down barriers of personal thought – as though realms of mysteries were open to us for expansion and liberation.

And yet! Are we free? Are we exhilarated, flowing in this stream of life, this ocean of the Spirit?

Are we conscious of the source of these new possibilities, or even grateful to these other kingdoms for their bondage and service to us?

Or (on the other hand) do we act like spoiled children crying for more and more toys and for the very moon itself? What can we really ever do with anything we have if we have no consciousness of it and no relation to it; if that subtle but powerful essence which binds all things together and makes them all children of Itself is to find no place in our hearts and in our minds!

Has not Bahá'u'lláh said that we are like the whales living in and upon the substance of the sea – without consciousness of that, which supports them and gives them life?

Where is our Oneness so eagerly offered us by Bahá'u'lláh for *our growth and advancement*, if we neglect to meditate and to attempt to relate ourselves – not only through action but by our very lives, the fourfold plan of our very being – which manifests in the outer, through form and action and within us as attitude and thought.

It is (it seems to me) that our minds and hearts must be unlocked and through these doors, *the vista*, wherein the vision of unity lies, will disclose to us our true relationship one to another and also not to be excluded, the mystery of our differences.

For the inner and outer states are both aspects of the One Life – and in the great vision of the Oneness of the World of Humanity we must look to the One Power manifesting these multitudinous divisions of Its one rich *Unity* so that we *may be stirred* to the wonder and majesty of Itself, and in this power of Cohesion we may get our first glimpse of the Unity and Universality of God.

What expansion! What rivers of inspiration pour from the greatness of Bahá'u'lláh's Being as He attempts to acquaint us with this vision of Oneness, this sublimity of the One Great Power!

It is, as though from every leaf and doorway, from every cloud and flower, from the mystery of sun and shadow, rain and heat – multiple mystic voices poured into His Heart the Glories of God. It is as though His eye beheld and knew the mystery hidden by the ardour of Its own manifestation!

How He laments! How the sacred pen weeps that our capacity is not able to receive more! What a grief must be His, as He feels all things turned back upon Himself as though the confines of His very being would break when there is no ear to hearken, no heart to receive these poems of the spirit!

Had He found us as we had been created, He could have disclosed mysteries which would have turned this world into a paradise!

But we imprison Him, the Radiant One, the Sun of Truth.

We, in our separate compartments of life, we shut him up in a prison of darkness, forgetful that the Sun of Truth knows no darkness, accepts no limitations!

But this Spiritual Sun burns through the confines of our world of thought even as the sun's rays fill valley and plain, flooding the high places and the low places with its light!

But in time we become oppressed, imprisoned in our dark towers of personal tragedies. In time we become surfeited with our little ways and something within us yearns and grows restless. Then we open the doors of our little dwellings and venture forth, perhaps quite unconscious as to what the spiritual season may be. For we have grown fretful under the weight of old thought and quite as naturally as when spring comes followed by summer we abandon our winter clothing for lighter wear – just so perhaps some hint of a new springtime has entered our mind and so we come forth out of our wintry hibernation to find ourselves upon the threshold of a new day – a new time spiritually – a time in which we are stirred to abandon the thought of the past and to find ourselves standing in the charged silence of *a new dawn.* The promise of light and beauty shines upon us, this promise a growing reality as it manifests itself in the action of the morning hours, the quiescence of high noon, when the sun seems to govern everything and all things are held in its powerful embrace of light!

Then the afternoon passes with the radiance of art and music, as though the day itself wove the garments of its own time – the long, long shadows begin to fall, bringing the last meditations of those who are still able to reflect the last rays of the setting sun in order to remember through the long night which comes to brood over us again.

And that, which so stirred us in the early days of Its light, seems to sink within us and we visit the tombs of what once was. And some forget that another Dawn will come, and some deny, and we dig our graves of material civilization and enter the tombs of self forgetfulness.

'And those that forgot God, God made them to forget themselves!'

But in the long hours before the rising again of a new Sun of Truth, when all have forgotten and men are asleep upon their beds of negligence, there are some who remember – such men as Shaykh Aḥmad and Siyyid Káẓim – and they speak and foretell prophesies of the return of God's promise, and in that magic hour a new Sun appears, a new Dawn floods the skies, tints the ashen clouds o'er land and sea, clinging unto the mountains and trees, a bodyless spirit embracing as a lover all contingent forms and in this embrace *of the Return* all things are restored to the secret of life and the quickening of the lover's touch brings a great gladness and all become robed anew in a mantle of light. The joy of recognition spreads until no longer will strangers walk with covered heads but faces will be uplifted to recognize each other in the one Light of a new Day.

Plate 14 *Untitled* 1968. Monotype. Private Collection

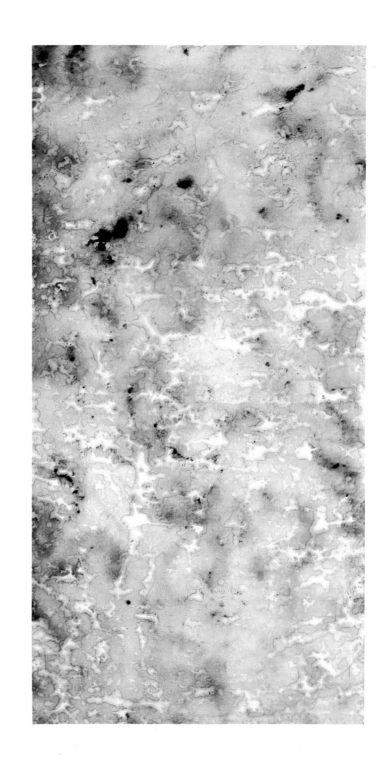

Plate 15 *Untitled* 1968. Monotype.
Collection Arthur L. Dahl and Joyce Lyon Dahl

POEMS

by

Mark Tobey

Where are the images
the magic hand
once drew?
In brown ink fire,
in rising lines of flame
upon some simple plane
of white, of yellow.
A pad at hand
communicating to an
artist fellow.

It is as though
the wind had stilled itself
to sleep – as though
the sun, its golden rays
each day forgot to reap.

I wonder
will the magic hand
again awake
and to
the artist fellow
in lines of fiery ink
again
communicate.

———————

When should the heart break
in the dining car
before a white clothed table
upon which
glitter and sparkle
silver and glass.

Or
should it break
and fall
into an open book
where
lovers meet and part
to be
closed up
put away
forgotten
like a pressed flower.
Or in the street
when
the evening light
punctuated by faintly glowing orbs
of golden yellow
tell one
how beautiful
light is.
Or
the evening is:
the street, the buildings, shops, signs,
they too
accented
with hurrying faces
and still more
hurrying eyes.

Why should the heart break
when all is well.
It doesn't.
It's sealed over
covered over
with meat and fish
and the well browned
English potato;
perhaps uncovered
beneath
suet pudding
upon which
gleams
streams of golden syrup
and
the chair is soft
before the evening fire;
while without
the winds cry
redolent
with historic memories.

History may be short or long
it doesn't matter
when the heart wants to break
to cry out, to know
to be defeated
crushed
lost forever
in the explosion
of multitudinous toy balloons
or terrified
frozen with fear
when gazed upon
by blazing eyes

of thousands of paper dragons,
but it doesn't happen.

You can beat your heart
with a hammer
you can cover it with tears
your love may slash it
with the keen cruel knives
of separation . . .
gossip may nibble
on its beautiful red outlines
(what joy to withered lips)
but it won't break
although at times
it seems so close
to breaking;
breaking
as waves break
ceaselessly
repeating
repeating . . .
. . . .

O break my heart
What form
the waves
when once
the shore is reached.

Portrait

You are as a dead thing living . . .
One from the mountains, walking in the valleys,
And your face has the sadness of pale, imprisoned moons.

You are like a white lotus, floating upon an opal sea,
Men dream of you, but do not find you,
Your path lies alone, strewn with stars.

Your eyes have the knowledge of dead and distant worlds,
Your hands are pale and lifeless, like the tiny white
      flowers in a child's dream:
The movement of your body is like the breathing of reflection
      in an unknown lake,
And upon your hair, no shadows fall.

O! remain not by the fountain of Human Sorrow;
The joys others seek, are not for you.
Return! Return! unto the worlds from whence you came!

Lily

You who are like a lily in a garden of white moonlight,
With head uplifted you stand motionless and secret.
Winds do not rise to disturb your perfume
And no bee finds its way into your golden heart:
The moon and stars are jealous of your chastity –
For their eyes have looked upon you,
But you are the purity of the night, untouched and unknown.
The restless waters of the fountain leap high that they may behold
      you mirrored in their silvery bodies;
The beauty of the night is yours and you answer in the majesty
      of your silence.

Plate 16 *No Space Left* 1965. Tempera. $34\frac{1}{4} \times 22$.
Private Collection

Time Structures

Remembering
Desiring to Remember
Thru wood and stone
In jade and light imprisoned crystal of this earth
They carved their path.

To keep alive and count the thread
Of passing time
To keep alive the seconds
Formed of Light.
The sacredness of memory
The secret call
O! Devotee of devotion
Bringing all to sacred contemplation.

Forms upon forms
The Buddha rises
Lifting thru
Time dreamed concepts
Set in Stone, in wood,
In jade and light imprisoned crystals of earth,
Speaking in Elegant Silence
Of the Resting place of Minds,
Of hearts united.

O Higher Universal
Reflected in Creations Time
Thru races set apart by names
By minds unenchanted
O! lights,
You rise again and yet again
Knower of Names, creating fire
Burning the hearts laden with snow
Deep in forgetfulness.

Oh! enchanting lights, oh! gentle
Winds of morning, the leaves know
They touch and speak thy will, and
Move in Praise of thee.

Thou bringest dreams to me and
In this life, their dream, they fashioned
Them in stone and wood, in jade and
Light imprisoned forms of earth's remembrance.

Oh! Universal Light. Oh! Mother of the Earth.
Some day, when all remember
The forms no more shall rise
In stone and earth
But in their substance
Shall be built of light.

The eye of the desert opens to the hollow cry of death.
The space yawns in the fierce glow of sunset.
The line of demarcation grows thin between being and not being.
The eye burns gold, burns crimson and fades to ash.

The eye burns gold, burns crimson and fades to ash.
The thunder is gone, reverberating in the hollows beyond lost hills.
Contentment is forever, or for never.

Contentment is forever, or for never.

The apple is red,
red forever the leaves where memory, like water,
seeps and sinks,
ever beyond two layers,
unnoticed and unobserved.
The horns of autumn are lifted beyond the woods,
compelling and sweet.
The frost moves, covers and bites in silence.
September sends down to us its message,
a yellow leaf in whirling ecstasy,
before sleep, before death.
The dragon fly lights on the grey bark of tree
and is gone to some distant point of sky.
Where does the round moon live?

Where does the round moon live?
Are the trees afire in the crimson sunset?
The eye is seen and remembered through other eyes.
The horizons are numberless as falling drops of rain.
The eye opens,
the first silent movement of the day.
The eyes are not related in unison.

The eyes are not related in unison.
The circle is too small.
It binds and bruises.
Even the agony is restricted.
Thoughts can be round.

Thoughts can be round, as the moon is round,
as man seeks man,
as brother is known to brother.
Man in wholeness, man in roundness,
a round world.

53

Plate 17 *Forest Fire* 1956. Tempera. 12×18. Collection Arthur L. Dahl

RECOLLECTIONS

by

Marion Hofman

Except for some weeks in the early 1940s, when Mark Tobey stayed and painted in the home of Dr Mildred Nichols in San Francisco, a house which I then shared, my meetings with him were infrequent but always memorable. Desiccated, as I often felt, by pressure of work – 'flattened out' in an almost literal sense – these contacts with his creative spirit renewed one's own life force and restored the contours of one's inmost nature. Although he himself was often inundated by feelings at odds with each other – 'my active and passive natures resist one another often ending in a deadlock', he wrote in 1938 – one never ceased to be affected by his creativity which moved within him like an irrepressible bubbling spring of fresh water, a veritable water of life with which true artists have ever renewed the spiritual nature of man and, thus, his culture.

That his art – and, how much more, his presence – did indeed impart such a spirit is mirrored in these words from a review by Michel Ragon of the retrospective exhibition at the Louvre in 1961. 'His art, though unassuming, is nonetheless a continual dialogue with the spirit. These are the Tablets of the Law whose indecipherable writing often moves us like messages from another world.'

I had heard much of Mark Tobey, and to meet him for the first time at the Geyserville Bahá'í Summer School in 1938 was truly exciting. My love and admiration for him date from those few days. But more exciting was to see him at work in Dr Nichols's house. Each morning she and I would go into the city, and each night on our return we would find some picture further advanced. I recall how he would begin with a canvas which he had filled with a kind of undifferentiated ethereal cloud, and from this and within it he picked out each day some form, some exquisite, delicate colour, gradually shaping his picture as, I imagined, God must have shaped the world. I recognized several of those paintings in the Paris retrospective.

Another vivid memory is of Mark at the 1943 Geyserville Bahá'í School, when he spoke, during the second week of a course, on 'The Oneness of Mankind'. It had been a course so integrated in its plan that it bombarded our intellects and emotions, until the intensity of our reactions had mounted almost unbearably. I can never forget how, with his opening words, Mark unloosed all our strain and reduced all of us to an uncontrollable and healing laughter which quite 'stopped the show'.

It was during this School, too, that I witnessed Mark's restlessness and a unique alleviation of it. One afternoon, needing to escape from the School for a few hours, he asked me to drive him to Healdsburg, a small town – but much larger than Geyserville – a few miles away. There we parked, and he wandered the streets, looking in shop windows, commenting, talking, until we came to a hardware store, and here he entered. From counter to counter he went, picking up various objects and examining them. All at once he came upon a very large iron nail. It spoke to him, delighted him; he bought it, and we returned happily and at peace to Geyserville.

I did not see Mark often after that since I moved to England in 1945, but through the kindness of friends I was kept in touch with his career which, at long last, was beginning to mount to its high success. Catalogues of various exhibitions and newspaper clippings reached me from time to time. It gave me much satisfaction to read a summing up of his retrospective show in the spring of 1951 at the California Palace of the Legion of Honor by the distinguished critic from the *San Francisco Chronicle* who had been extremely negative about Mark's earlier exhibition in the same gallery: '... the painting is achieved with the most brilliant technical command, with infallible sensitivity, and with a fusion of skill and insight such as is possessed only by a major master of art and craft.' (8 April 1951)

The remarkable scope, diversity and beauty of Mark Tobey's artistic achievement was revealed, at long last and in his seventieth year, at the Paris retrospective exhibition. Others have described this unforgettable occasion and its opening in the presence of eminent men who honoured our distinguished Bahá'í. For Bahá'í Mark always was, openly for public knowledge, in all his catalogues and interviews, never disguising what he owed to the inspiration of Bahá'u'lláh, nor what mankind owes in this new age just opening. 'If people would only take the time to investigate the writings of Bahá'u'lláh they would find the answers . . .', he wrote at the opening of a section of excerpts from his own writing which is included in the handsome catalogue of that exhibition.

I was privileged to see something of Mark's humility and dedication to Bahá'u'lláh, when on the second day of the exhibition, as I was sitting alone to read his catalogue, he came and sat with me. Here, in his hour of triumph in the world, with a great enlargement of his name in his own handwriting surmounting the entrance from the rue de Rivoli, he spoke wistfully of his life as an artist in comparison with a life of direct and active service in the Faith. 'But you have raised the flag of the Faith high in the world,' I exclaimed. It was only in succeeding years that I heard, too, of his generous gifts to Bahá'í pioneers and of his support of Bahá'í institutions, now that fame enabled him to be a benefactor.

How much one could write, how much in future will be written of this dear, gentle and kindly man, and of his distinctive contribution to the birth of a spiritual and universal art. But for this small essay let his own words from 1945 conclude: 'New seeds are no doubt being sown which mean new civilizations and, let us hope, cultures too. If I do anything important in painting some age will bring it forth and understand . . . Shall we, as we view the increasingly darkening sky, not hope for a Byzantium, some spot to keep alight the cultural values? For what else shall we live?'

MARK TOBEY

A Letter and Two Snapshots

by

Roger White

It is one thing to paint a picture, and another to experience it. Mark Tobey

24 April 1976
Haifa

I came along too late to know you well, Mark –
geography and our ages against it, an ocean between –
so, learning of your death, I sift for photographs
and memory serves up only two.
Others must have many; I am content with mine.
Both speak to me of courage: you will not find that strange.

The Temple in Wilmette is background to the first.
It was 1953, in spring. I came,
new to conferences and the House of Worship,
excited, claiming it all, drunk with seizure.
You were on the stairs looking curiously lonely in the
            bubbling crowd.
I saw the wistfulness.
Someone whispered your name and I broke away,
rushing at you in adolescent ebullience,
bristling to possess my first celebrity.
You were a Bahá'í – public – mine
like the Temple and the nine-pointed star.
I saw your momentary wince,
the flash of what I knew to be
a customary irritability,
saw you as a victim, as target, as too often possessed
and made, trivially, an unwilling familiar.
Meetings and martyrs are of many kinds.
In that moment I could have wept for your vulnerability.

What name do we give the process
that translates private pain into human service?
We clutch the ready cliché 'he did the Bahá'í thing'
and hope we're understood.
I do not know what need you read in me
but instantly you took that step,
leaned towards my abashment.
I cannot measure your cost,
saw only the warm smile,
the reaching out, the bestowal of the gift.
You would have me be your fellow-conspirator,
pretended rescuer, playmate for Peck's bad boy.
'Let's escape and have some tea', you said,
and led me away, appointing me your shield,
feigning to be led. The crowd would have held you
but for the perfection of your pantomime:
two established friends
hastening through the jostle
to the deserved privacy of a longstanding, self-promised tryst,
the venerable one acknowledging greetings on the fly,
the younger appearing the more eager to be off.
Do not suggest it was mere expediency –
we know when we are used.

The stratagem succeeded.
Companionably seated in the café, in snug anonymity,
I was dizzy with expectation: what would be revealed?
Soon I knew.
You spoke of the weather in Seattle,
            the food in Switzerland,
            of arthritis,
            of growing old.
And not a word about painting or the Faith.
I was not long puzzled. In that pedestrian flow
I was given access: Mark Tobey was revealed.
You *are* a painter – you *paint*: there, on canvas, your words.

You *are* a Bahá'í: befriending the young stranger,
offering tea, presenting the Faith in *transaction.*
Even then I was grateful to be spared discipleship
and a gratuitous verbal tour of those landmarks
that trace the outermost fringes of the stronghold of belief,

or a recital of those polite bywords we erect as barriers
at the remotest courtyard of identity
to discourage rather than invite entry or homecoming.

We separated smoothly; I, your debtor, not made to feel one.
It was as though we had spoken many times
and grown secure in our partings.

More than twenty years have passed; the picture does
               not fade.
I have my own Mark Tobey, unretouched,
and often I consult it when courage is the prize.
I would not trade it and no, Mark, it is not for sale.

London, 1963: spring again, the Jubilee,
another picture, an even larger crowd.
I did not look for you among the thousands but
found myself seated again at tea with you
in a random gathering,
you winking playful recognition of a long-ago ruse.
When, by chance, we were alone
you spoke of the weather in London,
             the food in France,
             of arthritis
             of growing old,
             of loneliness.
Again I was not puzzled:
By then had seen your paintings, had trembled,
had heard and seen you in the white writing,
knew your themes, your swoon.

'Martyrs are not popular subjects', you once remarked.
I did not ask why you painted martyrs, Mark,
though I marvelled at your valour.
Martyrs bear witness to belief;
they are the supreme lovers;
they die for love.
Who would paint martyrs in an age that debases the word
to a tag of parlour-game psychology?
Who would dare paint love in a world that has forgotten it?
Who, indeed, would frame and hang his soul?

Plate 18 *Conflict of the Satanic and Celestial Egos*
1918. Watercolour. $18\frac{1}{2} \times 12$. Private Collection,
Seattle

Plate 19 *The Middle West* 1929. Oil. $37\frac{3}{4} \times 59\frac{3}{4}$. The Seattle Art Museum, gift of Mrs D. Stimson, 42.20

Plate 20 *Three Birds* 1935. Watercolour, gouache. $10\frac{3}{4} \times 14\frac{7}{8}$. The Seattle Art Museum, Eugene Fuller Memorial Collection, 36.42

Plate 21 *Table and Ball* 1936. Tempera. 10½×19½. The Seattle Art
Museum, Eugene Fuller Memorial Collection, 36.403

Plate 22 *Seated Japanese Figure* 1934. Ink. 14¾×11½. The Seattle Art
Museum, Eugene Fuller Memorial Collection, 40.67

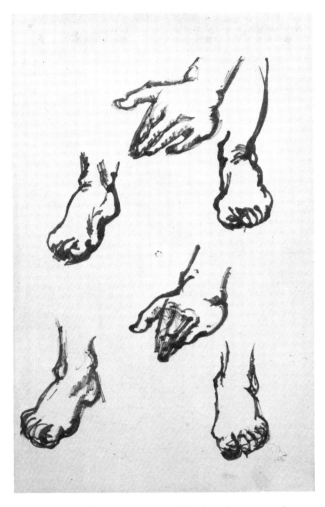

Plate 23 *Hands and Feet* 1955. Ink drawing. 12×18½.
Collection Arthur L. Dahl and Joyce Lyon Dahl

Plate 24 *Two Seated Figures* 1955. Ink drawing. 20¼×16¼.
Private Collection

Plate 25 *Portrait of Paul McCoole* 1925. Conte crayon. 24×18¼.
The Seattle Art Museum, bequest of Mrs Thomas D. Stimson,
63.105

Plate 26 *Portrait of Pehr Hallsten* 1942. Pastel. 21¾×15¾.
Collection of Arthur L. Dahl and Joyce Lyon Dahl

Plate 27 *Worker* 1943. Tempera. 43×25

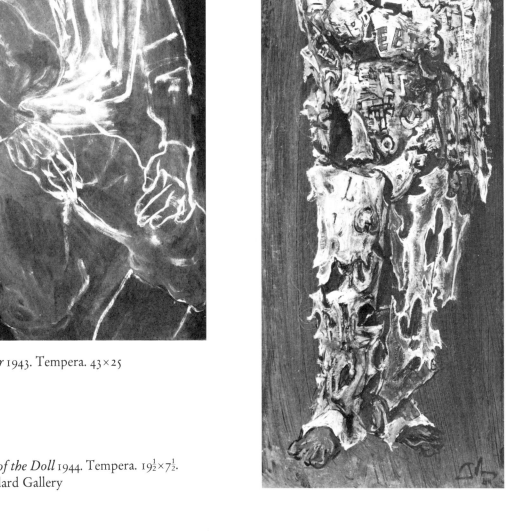

Plate 28 *Voice of the Doll* 1944. Tempera. $19\frac{1}{2}\times7\frac{1}{2}$.
Collection Willard Gallery

Plate 29 *Self Portrait* 1952. Tempera. 13¾×11. Gift of Joyce Lyon Dahl, Stanford University Museum of Art

Plate 30 *Imperator* 1944. Tempera. 16⅜×12¼. Private Collection

Plate 31 *Three Market Men* 1944. Tempera. 24×19.
Private Collection

Plate 32 *Market Figure* Ink and watercolour. $8\frac{1}{4}×5\frac{1}{2}$.
Private Collection

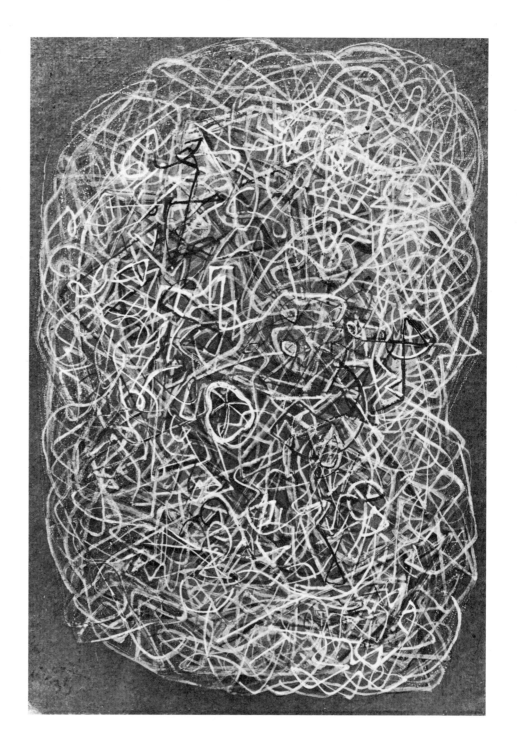

Plate 33 *Broadway Norm* 1935. Tempera.
$13\frac{1}{4} \times 9\frac{3}{8}$. Private Collection

Plate 34 *Forms Follow Man* 1941. Tempera. $13\frac{5}{8} \times 19\frac{5}{8}$. The Seattle Art Museum, Eugene Fuller Memorial Collection, 50.90

Plate 35 *The Void Devouring the Gadget Era* 1942. Tempera. $21\frac{1}{2} \times 29\frac{3}{8}$. The Museum of Modern Art, New York, gift of the artist

Plate 36 *Rummage* 1941. Watercolour,
gouache. $38\frac{3}{8} \times 25\frac{7}{8}$. The Seattle Art Museum,
Eugene Fuller Memorial Collection, 42.28

Plate 37 *Gothic* 1943. Tempera. $27\frac{3}{4} \times 21\frac{5}{8}$.
The Seattle Art Museum, bequest of
Berthe Poncy Jacobson, 75.35

Plate 38 *Pacific Transition* 1943. Gouache. $23\frac{1}{4} \times 31\frac{1}{4}$. The St. Louis Art Museum, gift of Joseph Pulitzer Jr.

Plate 39 *New Day* 1945? Tempera. $12\frac{3}{8} \times 23\frac{1}{8}$. Courtesy of the Archives of the National Spiritual Assembly of the Bahá'ís of the United States

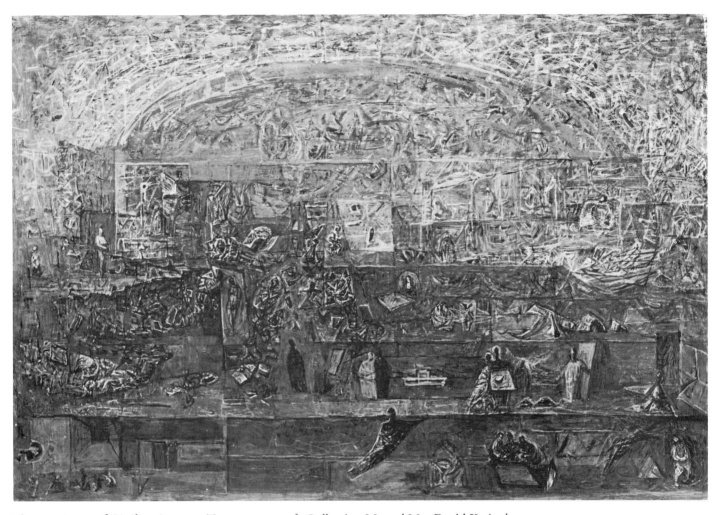

Plate 40 *Arena of Civilization* 1947. Tempera. 14×19¾. Collection Mr and Mrs David K. Anderson

Plate 41 *Jacob and the Angel* 1949. Tempera.
$12\frac{1}{8} \times 7\frac{3}{8}$. Gift of Joyce Lyon Dahl, Stanford
University Museum of Art

Plate 42 *Concourse* 1943. Tempera. $10\frac{1}{4} \times 14\frac{1}{4}$. Collection Joyce Lyon Dahl

Plate 43 *Day of the Martyr* 1947. Tempera. 12×18. Collection Joyce Lyon Dahl

Plate 44 *Biography* 1948. Tempera. $10\frac{1}{2} \times 7\frac{1}{4}$. Gift of Joyce Lyon Dahl, Stanford University Museum of Art

Plate 45 *New York* 1944. Tempera. 33×21.
National Gallery of Art, Washington DC, gift
of the Avalon Foundation, 1976

Plate 46 *Agate World* 1945. Water-colour, gouache. $14\frac{7}{8} \times 11$. The Seattle Art Museum, gift of the Eunice P. Clise Fund, The Seattle Foundation, 50.110

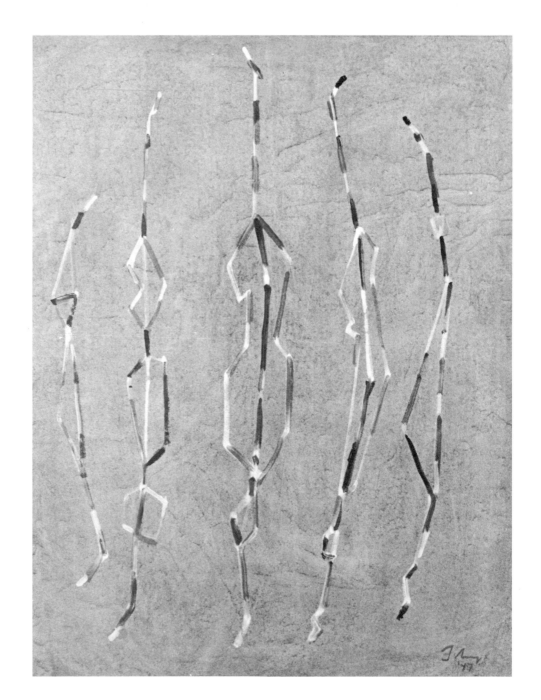

Plate 47 *Five Dancers* 1947. Tempera.
$23\frac{3}{4} \times 18\frac{1}{2}$. Private Collection

Plate 48 *Space Intangibles* 1949. Tempera. 28×44. Museum of Art, Ogunquit

Plate 49 *Remote Field* 1944. Tempera, pencil and crayon. $28\frac{1}{8} \times 30\frac{1}{8}$. The Museum of Modern Art, New York, gift of Mr and Mrs Jan de Graff

Plate 50 *Archaic Satire* 1948.
Tempera. 25×19. Collection
Harold and Marzieh Gail

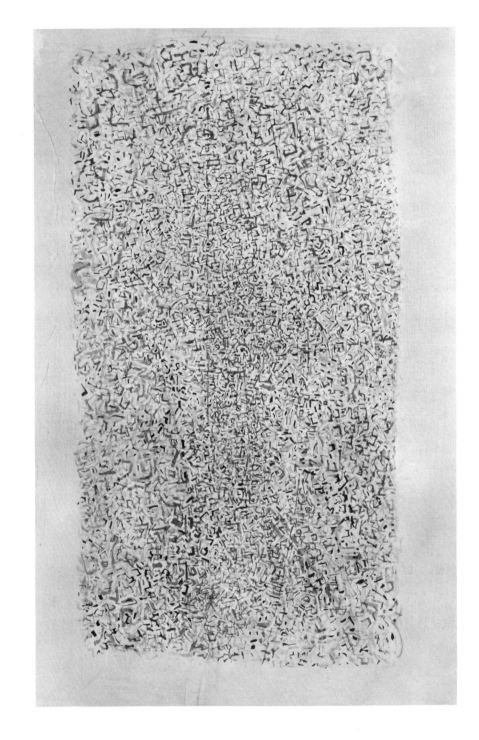

Plate 51 *Universal City* 1951. Watercolour,
gouache. $37\frac{1}{2} \times 25$. The Seattle Art Museum, gift
of Mr and Mrs Dan Johnson, 70.89

Plate 52 *Universal Field* 1949. Pastel and tempera. 28×44. Collection of the Whitney Museum of American Art, purchase, acquisition no. 50.24

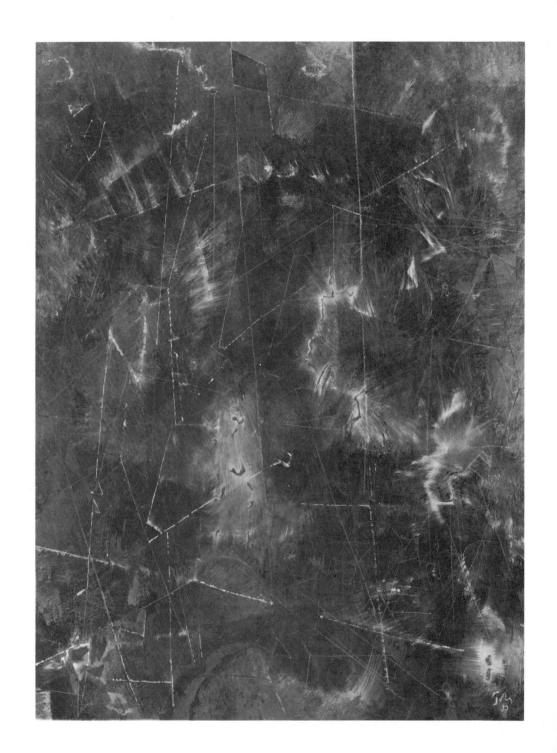

Plate 53 *Above the Earth* 1953.
Gouache. $39\frac{1}{2} \times 29\frac{3}{4}$. Collection of
the Art Institute of Chicago

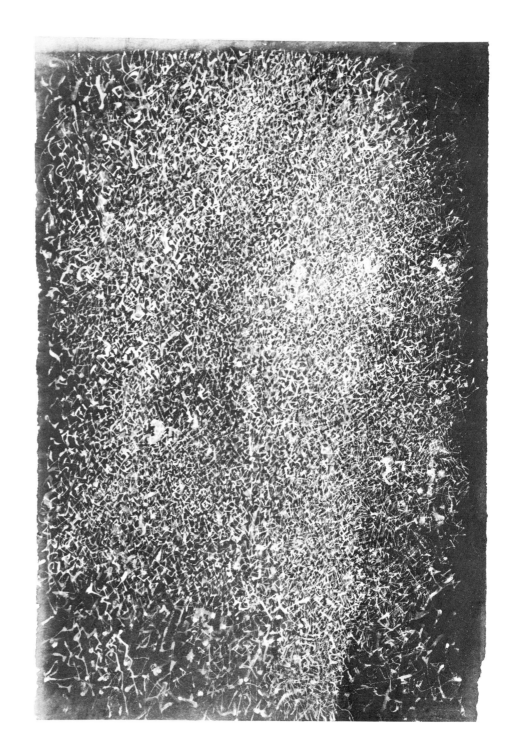

Plate 54 *Meditative Series VIII* 1954.
Tempera. $17\frac{7}{8} \times 11\frac{7}{8}$. Private Collection

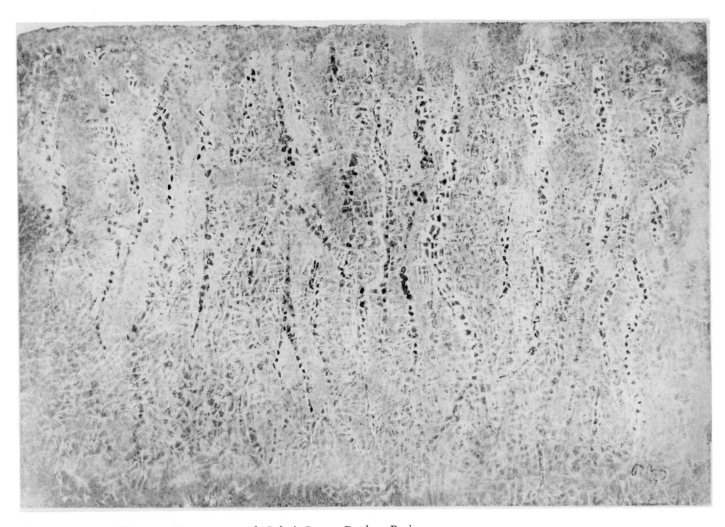

Plate 55 *Pattern Africa* 1954. Tempera. $7 \times 10\frac{3}{4}$. Galerie Jeanne Bucher, Paris

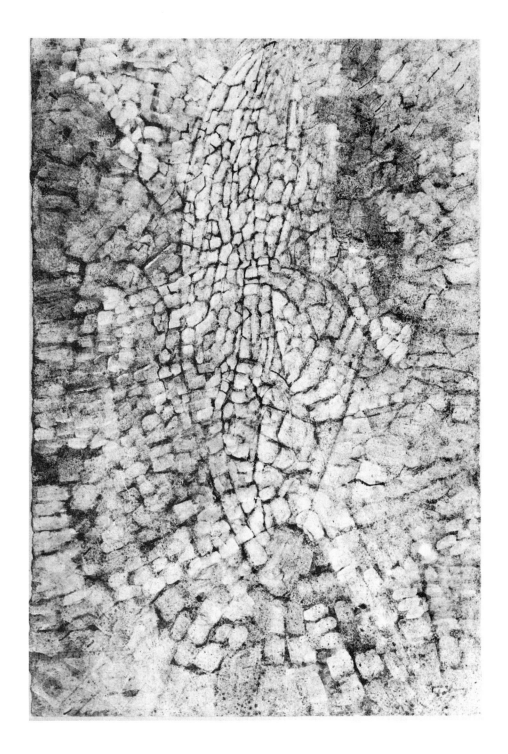

Plate 56 *Wing* 1954. Tempera. $17 \times 11\frac{1}{2}$.
Private Collection

Plate 57 *Animal Kingdom* 1954. Tempera. $5\frac{1}{8} \times 8\frac{7}{8}$. Gift of Joyce Lyon Dahl, Stanford University Museum of Art

Plate 58 *New World Dimensions II* 1954. Tempera. $11\frac{3}{4} \times 17\frac{3}{4}$. Courtesy of the Archives of the National Spiritual Assembly of the Bahá'ís of the United States

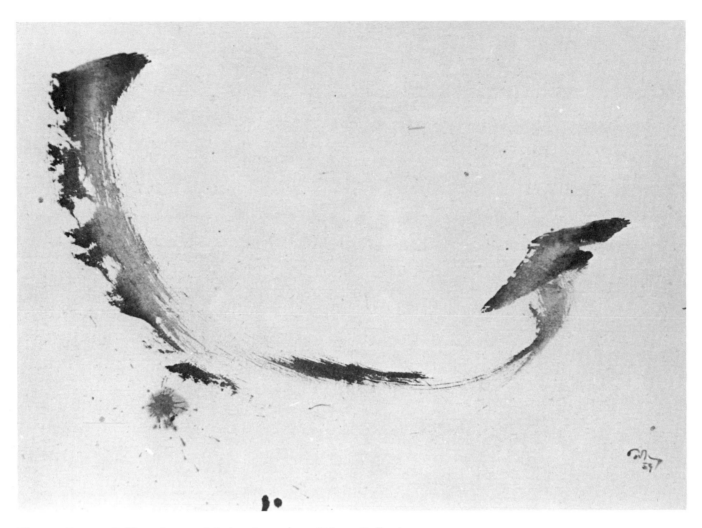

Plate 59 *Eastern Calligraphy* 1959. Ink drawing. $14\frac{1}{2} \times 20$. Private Collection

Plate 60 *Sumi IX* 1957. Ink drawing. $22\frac{3}{4} \times 33\frac{3}{4}$. Collection Arthur L. Dahl and Joyce Lyon Dahl

Plate 61 *Sumi II* 1957. Ink Drawing. $20\frac{1}{2} \times 28\frac{3}{4}$. Private Collection

Plate 62 *Fire Dance* 1957. Ink drawing. 21 × 28. Gift of Joyce Lyon Dahl, Stanford University Museum of Art

Plate 63 *Sumi I* 1957. Ink drawing. $22\frac{3}{4} \times 34\frac{1}{4}$. Gift of Joyce Lyon Dahl, Stanford University Museum of Art

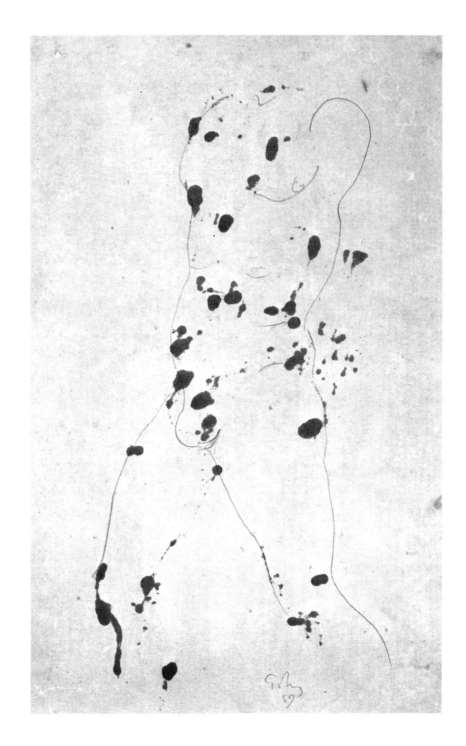

Plate 64 *Man's Torso with Spots* 1957. Ink and pencil. $12\frac{1}{2} \times 8$. Private Collection

Plate 65 *Still Life No. 3* 1958. 7¾×7. Gift of Joyce Lyon Dahl, Stanford University Museum of Art

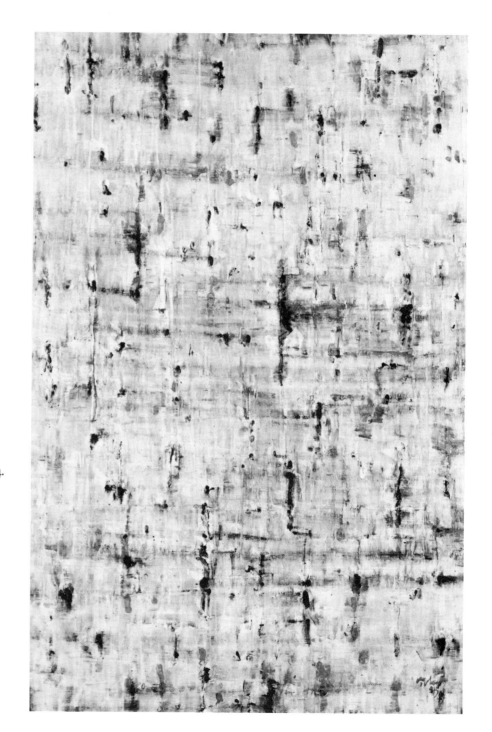

Plate 66 *Wounded Tide* 1957. Tempera. $35\frac{3}{4} \times 24$.
Collection Mr and Mrs Richard Lippold

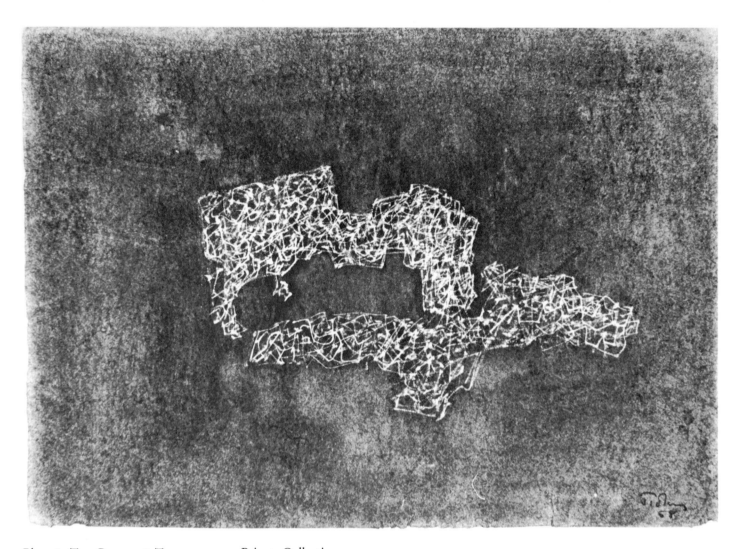

Plate 67 *Two Dogs* 1958. Tempera. 7 × 10. Private Collection

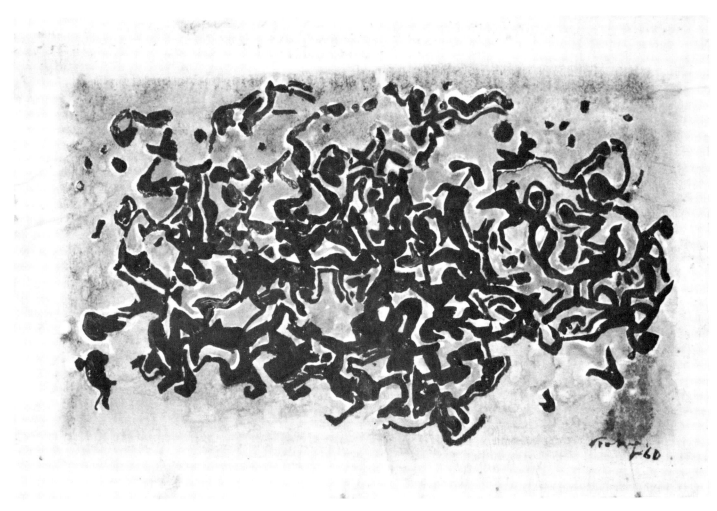

Plate 68 *Ancient Battle* 1960. Tempera. $4\frac{5}{8} \times 7\frac{1}{2}$. Collection Mrs Mary Ima, Seattle

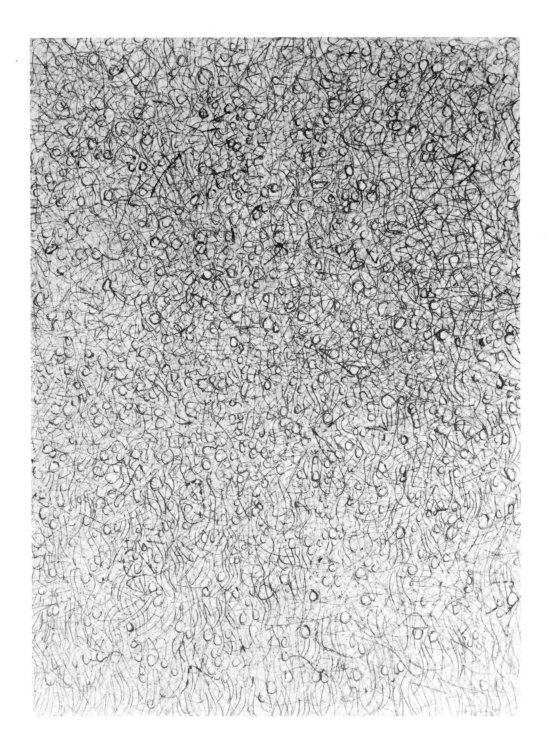

Plate 69 *Sentinels of the Field* 1958.
Coloured ink and tempera. $11\frac{3}{4}\times8\frac{7}{8}$.
Collection Joyce Lyon Dahl

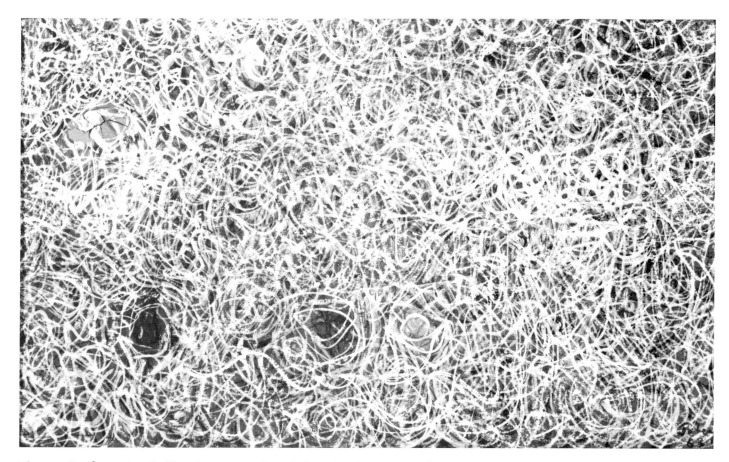

Plate 70 *Configurations in Transit* 1963. Casein and glue. $6\frac{1}{2} \times 10\frac{1}{2}$. Private Collection

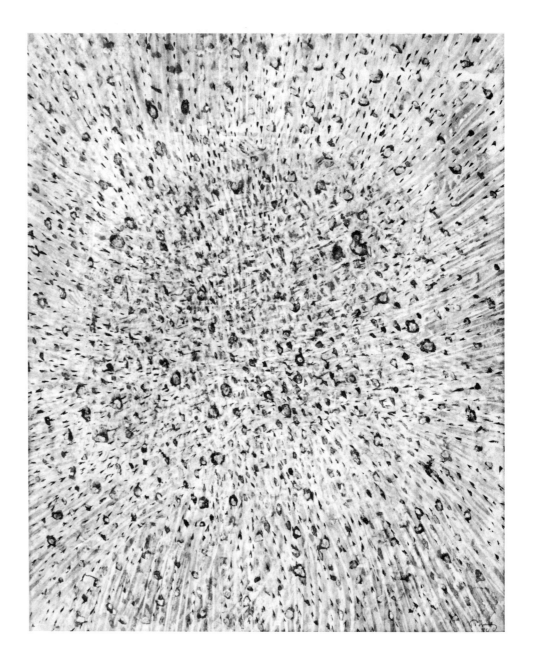

Plate 71 *New Genesis* 1958. Tempera.
$10\frac{3}{4} \times 8\frac{1}{4}$. Gift of Joyce Lyon Dahl,
Stanford University Museum of Art

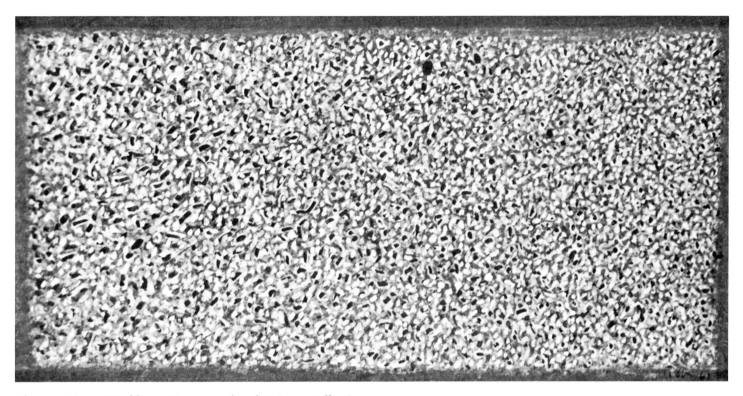

Plate 72 *Minute World* 1960. Tempera. $6\frac{1}{2} \times 13\frac{1}{4}$. Private Collection

Plate 73 *Traffic* 1959. Tempera. $6\frac{1}{2} \times 6\frac{1}{2}$. Gift of Joyce Lyon Dahl, Stanford University Museum of Art

Plate 74 *Serpentine* 1955. Watercolour, gouache and pencil. 29¾×39¾. The Seattle Art Museum, Silver Anniversary Fund, 50.114

Plate 75 *Magic Woods* 1962. Tempera.
$38\frac{1}{2} \times 29\frac{3}{8}$. Private Collection

Plate 76 *Blue Night* 1964. Tempera. $43\frac{1}{2} \times 27\frac{1}{4}$.
Private Collection

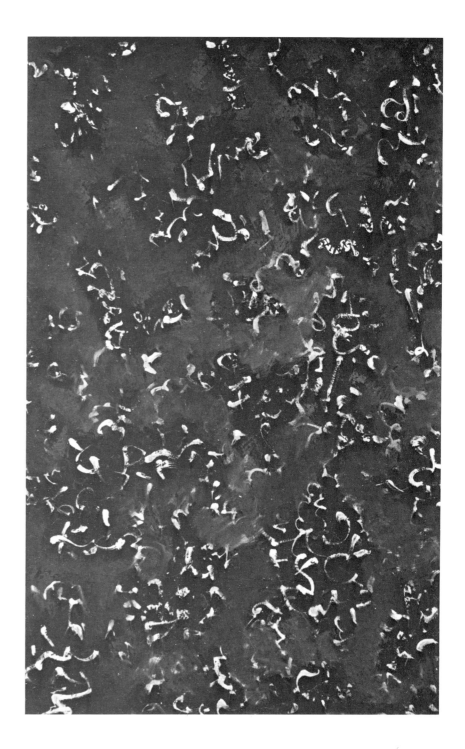

Plate 77 *Fastnacht* 1963. Tempera. $7\frac{1}{2} \times 11$. Private Collection

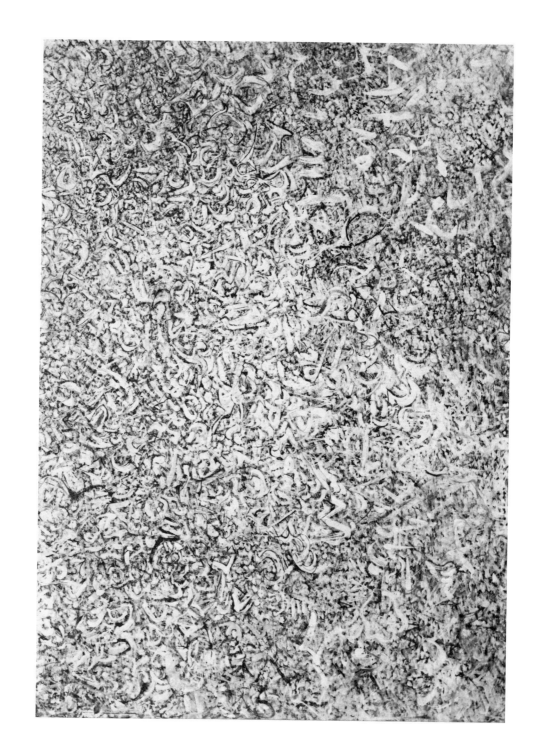

Plate 78 *Laughter in White* 1969.
Tempera. $42\frac{3}{4}\times31$. Private Collection

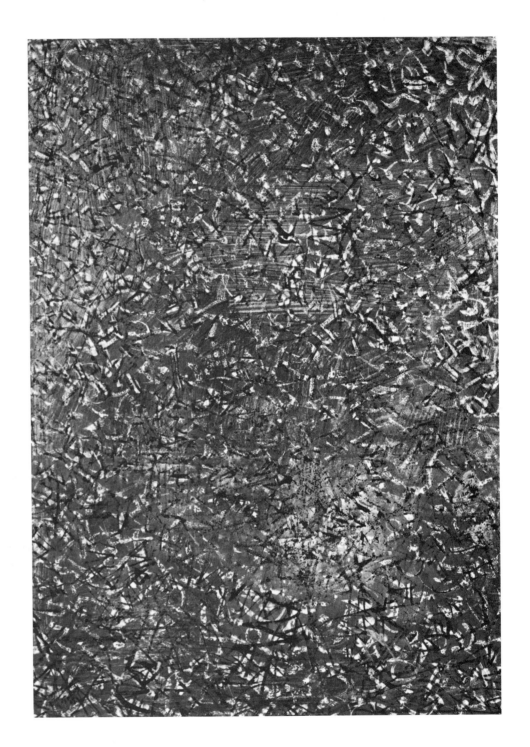

Plate 79 *Released* 1969. Tempera.
34×24. Private Collection

A SHORT READING LIST ON THE BAHÁ'Í FAITH

Bahá'í Scripture and Basic Texts

BAHÁÚ'LLÁH. *Gleanings from the Writings of Bahá'u'lláh.* Trans. by Shoghi Effendi, Wilmette, Illinois: Bahá'í Publishing Trust, 2nd rev. edn 1976.

—— *The Proclamation of Bahá'u'lláh.* Haifa: Bahá'í World Centre, 1967.

'ABDU'L-BAHÁ. *Foundation of World Unity.* Wilmette, Illinois: Bahá'í Publishing Trust, 1971.

—— *Paris Talks.* London: Bahá'í Publishing Trust, 11th edn 1969.

—— *Some Answered Questions.* A series of table talks on a wide variety of topics. Wilmette, Illinois: Bahá'í Publishing Trust, 1981.

SHOGHI EFFENDI. *Call to the Nations.* Extracts from his statements on World Order, Haifa: Bahá'í World Centre, 1977.

—— *God Passes By.* A history of the first century of the Bahá'í Faith. Wilmette, Illinois: Bahá'í Publishing Trust, 1965.

Biographies of the Three Central Figures

BALYUZI, H. M. *Bahá'u'lláh, The King of Glory.* Oxford: George Ronald, 1980.

—— *The Báb, The Herald of the Day of Days.* Oxford: George Ronald, 1974.

—— *'Abdu'l-Bahá, The Centre of the Covenant of Bahá'u'lláh.* Oxford: George Ronald, 1973.

Introductory Books

ESSLEMONT, J. E. *Bahá'u'lláh and the New Era.* An introduction to the history and teachings of the Bahá'í Faith, available in many languages. Wilmette, Illinois: Bahá'í Publishing Trust, 4th rev. edn 1975.

HOFMAN, DAVID. *The Renewal of Civilization.* A brief account of the history and teachings. Oxford: George Ronald, 1981.

HUDDLESTON, JOHN. *The Earth Is But One Country.* An analysis of the needs of mankind today, and how the Bahá'í Faith is contributing to the growth of a world-wide civilization. London: Bahá'í Publishing Trust, 1976.

TOWNSHEND, GEORGE. *The Promise of All Ages.* An introduction to the Bahá'í Faith of particular significance for Christians. Oxford: George Ronald.

Most of these titles are available in public and university libraries, or may be ordered from bookshops or directly from the publishers.

NOTES TO THE TEXT

MARK TOBEY, 1890–1976

1. William C. Seitz, *Mark Tobey*, New York, The Museum of Modern Art, 1962, p. 43.
2. Seitz, *ibid.*, p. 43.
3. Seitz, *ibid.*, p. 43.
4. Seitz, *ibid.*, p. 89.
5. Interview with Mark Tobey recorded by Arthur L. Dahl, 21 September 1963.
6. Seitz, *ibid.*, p. 44.
7. Letter from Doris Holley to Arthur L. Dahl, July 1976.
8. Seitz, *ibid.*, p. 45.
9. Janet Flanner, 'Tobey, mystique errant,' *L'Œil*, 15 June 1955. Reprinted in English in *Selective Eye*, New York, Random House, 1955.
10. Seitz, *ibid.*, p. 45.
11. Betty Bowen, exhibition catalogue, *Tobey's 80: A Retrospective*, Seattle Art Museum, University of Washington Press, 1970.
12. Mark Tobey, 'Reminiscence and Reverie', *Magazine of Art*, October 1951.
13. Seitz, *ibid.*, p. 47.
14. Tobey interview, *ibid.*, 1963.
15. Muriel Draper, 'Mark Tobey', *Creative Art*, October 1930.
16. Letter from Mark Tobey to Arthur and Joyce Dahl, 29 July 1955.
17. Letter from Mark Tobey to Arthur and Joyce Dahl, 26 April 1956.
18. Katharine Kuh, 'Through the Eyes of Mark Tobey', *Saturday Review/World*, 11 September 1973.
19. Quoted by Dorothy C. Miller, ed., *Fourteen Americans*, New York, The Museum of Modern Art, 1946, p. 70.
20. Virginia Barnett, address at funeral of Mark Tobey, 28 April 1976.

TOBEY'S WORLD VIEW

1. For this statement by Tobey see Dorothy C. Miller, ed., *Fourteen Americans*, New York, The Museum of Modern Art, 1946, p. 70. On the idea of 'roundness' in Tobey's painting see Dore Ashton, 'Mark Tobey et la rondeur parfaite', *XXe Siècle*, vol. 21, no. 12, May–June 1959, pp. 66-69. Miss Ashton points out references to roundness by Karl Jaspers, van Gogh, Joë Bousquet and La Fontaine, which are cited by the French philosopher Gaston Bachelard in *La Poétique de l'espace*, Paris, 1958, p. 208.
2. Mark Tobey, 'Reminiscence and Reverie', *Magazine of Art*, vol. 44, no. 6, Oct. 1951. This important article is abbreviated as *R & R* in subsequent notes.
3. *Bahá'í World Faith*, Wilmette, Bahá'í Publishing Trust, 1956, 2nd edn, p. 240.
4. *ibid.*, pp. 224-5.
5. *ibid.*, p. 228.
6. *ibid.*, p. 229.
7. Exhibition catalogue, Willard Gallery, New York, 1949.
8. Catalogue, Exhibition of Contemporary American Painting, University of Illinois, Urbana, 1950, p. 211.
9. For a comparison of Zen with Western philosophy and religion see William Barrett, 'Zen for the West', in D. T. Suzuki, *Zen Buddhism*, Garden City, Doubleday, 1956, pp. vii-xx.
10. *Bahá'í World Faith*, p. 236.
11. *ibid.*, p. 237.
12. 'Mark Tobey Writes of his Painting on the Cover', *Art News*, vol. 44, no. 18, 1-14, JAN 1946, p. 22.
13. Mark Tobey, comment in the files of the Willard Gallery.
14. *Bahá'í World Faith*, p. 170.
15. Mark Tobey, lecture at the Bahá'í Centre, New York, 30 October, 1951. Tobey is quoting from Shoghi Effendi, a grandson of Bahá'u'lláh.
16. In *Art News*, vol. 56, no. 4, summer 1956, p. 39.
17. Mark Tobey, excerpts from a letter, *The Tiger's Eye*, no. 3, 15 March 1948, p. 52.
18. *R & R*, p. 231.
19. Tobey quotes here from Bahá'u'lláh.
20. Mark Tobey, in a Bahá'í lecture, 1951 (see note 15).
21. Mark Tobey, *The Tiger's Eye*, p. 52 (see note 17).
22. B[elle] K[rasne], 'A Tobey Profile', *The Art Digest*, vol. 26, no. 2, 15 October, 1951, pp. 26, 34.
23. Robert Motherwell and Ad Reinhardt, eds., *Modern Artists in America*, New York, Wittenborn-Schultz, 1951: 'The Western Round Table on Modern Art' (1949), p. 30.
24. Denys Chevalier, 'Une journée avec Mark Tobey,' *Aujourd'hui*, vol. 6, no. 33, October 1961, p. 7.
25. *R & R*, p. 232.
26. Among the masters of whom Tobey speaks with admiration are Michelangelo, Raphael, Titian, Bronzino, El Greco, Holbein, Grünewald, Dürer, Rembrandt, Velazquez, Rubens, Guardi, Turner, Whistler, Monet, Cézanne, Inness, Liang K'ai, Mu-ch'i, Sesshu.
27. Krasne, *op. cit.*, p. 5.

28. Motherwell and Reinhardt, *op. cit.*, p. 28. The typescript of this session of 'The Western Round Table on Modern Art' (in The Museum of Modern Art Library) contains an unedited version of this statement).

29. Mark Tobey, from a comment in the files of the Willard Gallery, New York, on the painting *Tundra* (1944).

30. Statement in the files of the Willard Gallery, November 1942.

31. Mark Tobey, in *The Tiger's Eye*, p. 52 (see note 17).

THEMES AND SUBJECTS

1. Krasne, *op. cit.*, p. 34.

2. In 1960 Tobey worked on a large figure composition in oil, but abandoned it: 'To weld the figure into space and keep it so you can see it', he concluded, 'is almost impossible.'

3. *R & R*, p. 231.

4. Excerpt from a letter, 28 October, 1954. See *The Art Institute of Chicago Quarterly*, vol. 49, no. 1, 1 February, 1955, p. 9.

5. This comment has appeared in several slightly different versions; from the files of the Willard Gallery.

6. Mark Tobey, 'Japanese Traditions and Modern Art', *College Art Journal*, vol. **18**, no. 1, Fall 1958, p. 24.

7. Selden Rodman, *Conversations with Artists*, New York, Reynal and Hitchcock, 1944, p. 98.

8. Krasne, *op. cit.*, p. 26.

9. *R & R*, p. 229.

10. Exhibition catalogue, Willard Gallery, New York, 1949.

11. For an analysis of the stages in the mystical ascent see Evelyn Underhill, *Mysticism*, New York, Meridian, 1955 (1st edn 1910), pp. 167ff.

12. George Rowley, *Principles of Chinese Painting*, Princeton University Press, 1947, p. 4.

THE FRAGRANCE OF SPIRITUALITY

1. See, for instance, Alexander Watt, 'Paris Commentary', *The Studio*, December 1961, pp. 222-4 and 235.

2. Bahá'u'lláh and 'Abdu'l-Bahá. *Bahá'í World Faith*, Wilmette, Bahá'í Publishing Trust, 1956, p. 189.

3. *ibid.*, p. 377.

4. Mark Tobey, 'The Dot and the Circle', *World Order*, Vol. 14, no. 12, March 1949, pp. 412-416.

5. Tape-recorded conversation with Arthur L. Dahl, 1962.

6. Tobey, 'The Dot and the Circle'.

7. Letter to Arthur and Joyce Dahl, 26 April 1957, in *Mark Tobey: Paintings from the Collection of Joyce and Arthur Dahl*, Stanford, California, Stanford Art Book 7, 1967, p. 15.

8. Exhibition catalogue, Willard Gallery, New York, 1949.

9. Mark Tobey, Statement by the Artist', *Paintings by Mark Tobey*, Portland Art Museum, San Francisco Museum of Art, Detroit Institute of Arts, 1945-1946.

10. Stanford Art Book 7, p. 15.

11. *Mark Tobey*, Stedelijk Museum, Amsterdam, 1966, Catalogue no. 393.

12. Conversation with Arthur L. Dahl, 1962.

13. Tobey, 'Statement by the Artist'.

14. *Retrospective Exhibition Mark Tobey*, Whitechapel Gallery, London, 1962, pp. 11-12.

15. *Mark Tobey*, California Palace of the Legion of Honor, San Francisco, vol. 8, nos. 11-12, March-April 1951

16. Mark Tobey in Selden Rodman, *Conversations with Artists*, New York, Devin-Adair, 1957, p. 17.

17. Extract from a letter dated 1/2/55. Whitechapel catalogue, p. 13.

18. *Mark Tobey*, Musée des Arts Décoratifs, Palais du Louvre, Pavillon de Marsan, Paris, 1961, *and* Whitechapel catalogue, pp. 18-19.

19. Mark Tobey *in* Colette Roberts, *Mark Tobey*, New York, Grove Press, and London, Evergreen Books, 1959, p. 41.

20. Louvre catalogue *and* Whitechapel catalogue, pp. 18-19.

21. Mark Tobey, 'Art and Community', *World Order*, vol. 5, no. 1, April 1939, pp. 33-4.

22. Tobey *in* Roberts, pp. 41-42.

23. Julia and Lyonel Feininger, 'Comments by a fellow artist'. *Paintings by Mark Tobey*. Portland Art Museum, San Francisco Museum of Art, Detroit Institute of Arts, 1945-1946.

24. Mark Tobey *in* Betty Bowen, 'Introduction', *Tobey's 80, A Retrospective*, Seattle Art Museum, Seattle and London, University of Washington Press, 1970.

25. Letter to Marian Willard, October 1947, Louvre catalogue.

26. Letter from Mark Tobey to Arthur L. Dahl, 28 July 1966.

27. Whitechapel catalogue, p. 16.

28. *ibid.*, p. 21.

29. *ibid.*, p. 22.

30. Seitz, p. 31.

31. Letter to Arthur L. Dahl.

32. Whitechapel catalogue, p. 24.

33. Letter to Marian Willard, February 1953, Louvre catalogue.

34. Letter to Arthur L. Dahl, 7 May 1957, Stanford Art Book 7, p. 12

35. Whitechapel catalogue, p. 16.

36. Conversation with Arthur L. Dahl, 1962.

37. Conversation with Arthur L. Dahl, 1962, Stanford Art Book 7, p. 15.

INDEX OF PLATES

Page numbers in brackets indicate colour plates.